MCKENZIE'S FIGHTING FIFTH

First Order Book
of
the 5th Tennessee Cavalry Regiment
Confederate States of America

Transcribed by
Carl Campbell

Rhea County Historical and
Genealogical Society

Heritage Books
2024

HERITAGE BOOKS
AN IMPRINT OF HERITAGE BOOKS, INC.

Books, CDs, and more—Worldwide

For our listing of thousands of titles see our website
at
www.HeritageBooks.com

A Facsimile Reprint
Published 2024 by
HERITAGE BOOKS, INC.
Publishing Division
5810 Ruatan Street
Berwyn Heights, MD 20740

Rhea County Historical and
Genealogical Society
1999

— Publisher's Notice —
In reprints such as this, it is often not possible to remove
blemishes from the original. We feel the contents of this
book warrant its reissue despite these blemishes and
hope you will agree and read it with pleasure.

International Standard Book Number
Paperbound: 978-0-7884-8716-3

INTRODUCTION

The Fifth (McKenzie's) Tennessee Cavalry Regiment, Confederate States of America, was organized in Upper East Tennessee on December 16, 1862 with Col. George W. McKenzie as commander. However, the Regiment had its origin in earlier organizations and, as with many Confederate units, there is some confusion in the names by which it was known in the first years of the war. Dr. Lindsley did not include a history of the Regiment in his *Annals* and the following summary is based on the data published by the Tennessee Civil War Centennial Commission in 1964 and other general sources.

On August 24, 1861 a company of men from Hamilton County, Tennessee, North Alabama and North Georgia was mustered at Knoxville, Tennessee. It was commanded by John F. White (after his promotion by J. L. Blackwell and later by A. J. Reagan) and was designated Company F on January 7, 1862 (Company A, 5th Regiment).

On October 19, 1861 a company of men from Union County was mustered at Knoxville. It was commanded by A. J. Brock and was designated Company A on January 7, 1862.

On October 2, 1861 a company of men from Washington and Greene Counties was mustered at Knoxville. It was commanded by John B. McLin (after his promotion by William W. Mullendore) and was designated Company G on January 7, 1862 (Company H, 5th Regiment).

On November 1, 1861 a company of men from Meigs County was mustered at Decatur, Tennessee. It was commanded by George W. McKenzie (after his promotion by W. O. Martin and later by D. C. Blevins) and was designated Company B on January 7, 1862 (Company C, 5th Regiment).

On November 12, 1861 a company of men from Bradley County was mustered at Cleveland, Tennessee. It was commanded by William L. Brown and was designated Company C on January 7, 1862.

On November 13, 1861 a company of men from Polk County was mustered at Cleveland, Tennessee. It was commanded by Robert W. McClary (later by Thaddeus M. Carder) and was designated Company D on January 7, 1862 (Company E, 5th Regiment).

On November 20, 1861 a company of men from Cocke County was mustered at Knoxville. It was commanded by Thomas S. Gorman (later by A. L. Mims) and became Company E on January 7, 1862 (Company F, 5th Regiment).

The First Tennessee Cavalry Regiment was created on January 7, 1862 with these companies. Col. John Rogers (sometimes spelled Rodgers) was commander. John F. White of Company F became Lieutenant Colonel and J. L. Blackwell took command of White's company. The unit was referred to as First (Rogers') Tennessee Cavalry Regiment.

On January 27, 1862 a company of men from Roane, Meigs and McMinn Counties was mustered at Knoxville. It was commanded by James M. Kincaid (later by John Blythe) and became Company H in First (Rogers') Tennessee Cavalry Regiment (Company B, 5th Regiment).

On February 14, 1862 a company of men from Bradley County was mustered at Cleveland. It was commanded by John G. M. Montgomery and upon his promotion by Alvin W. Beagles (sometimes spelled Beegles). It became Company I in First (Rogers') Tennessee Cavalry Regiment (Company D, 5th Regiment).

On March 31, 1862 an independent company was mustered at Knoxville. It was commanded by William B. Jones (later by John W. Graham) and became Company K in First (Rogers') Tennessee Cavalry Regiment (Company G, 5th Regiment).

On April 12, 1862 Capt. A. J. Brock's Company A was mustered out of service, possibly because the authorities doubted its loyalty to the Confederacy. On May 16, William L. Brown's Company C transferred in a body to the 63rd Tennessee Infantry Regiment as Company H. This change most likely came about because the company had lost horses in a Federal raid and could not afford to replace them. With these two changes company letters A and C were vacated.

The First (Rogers') Tennessee Cavalry Regiment was reorganized on May 24, 1862 under the conscript act with eight companies. John B. McLin (formerly commander of Company G) replaced John Rogers as regimental commander. The unit was officially designated the Second (McLin's) Tennessee Cavalry Regiment but was sometimes still referred to as the First (Rogers') Regiment.

At this time the Regiment was brigaded with the First Georgia Regiment, the First (later Second) Regiment known as Ashby's Regiment, the Third (Starnes') Regiment, and Huwald's Battery. The Brigade was commanded by Col. Benjamin Allston.

On July 4, 1862 a company of men commanded by Dewitt C. Ghormley was mustered at Maryville, Tennessee as Company F of Thomas' North Carolina Legion.

On July 19, 1862 a company of men from Meigs and Hamilton Counties was mustered at Shiloh Church in Rhea County. It was commanded by William W. Lillard who had served as an officer in McKenzie's Company.

The Second (McLin's) Cavalry Regiment was reduced to a battalion on August 12, 1862 by order of Gen. Kirby Smith. McLin was replaced by George W. McKenzie and the unit was designated the Second Cavalry Battalion. Since there was already a Second Battalion, it was known officially as the 13th Battalion, although most often referred to as the Second.

On September 5, 1862 in General Order No. 1 Col. McKenzie ordered company letters changed: Blackwell's Company changed from F to A; Kincaid's from H to B; Martin's from B to C; Beagles' from I to D; Carder's from D to E; Mims' from E to F; Graham's from K to G; and Mullendore's from G to H.

On October 9, 1862 William W. Lillard's Company (mustered July 19) became Company I in the Battalion and retained that letter when the Battalion became the 5th Regiment.

Dewitt Ghormley's Company (mustered July 4) was transferred from Thomas' Legion and became Company K on December 16, 1862. Having ten companies, the battalion was restored to regimental status and designated the Fifth (McKenzie's) Tennessee Cavalry Regiment and known by that name for the remainder of the war.

Throughout its early history, this regiment served in East Tennessee in Allston's Brigade, then as a member of John B. Palmer's Brigade and later in John S. Scott's Brigade along with the Tenth Confederate Cavalry, the First Louisiana Regiment, the Second (Ashby's) Regiment, the 5th North Carolina Battalion and Marshall's Battery.

Until the summer of 1863 it was busy guarding the mountain passes, arresting bushwhackers, raiding into southeastern Kentucky, and skirmishing with Federal forces. At the evacuation of East Tennessee by the Confederates in August 1863, the Fifth Cavalry Regiment served as the rear guard of Buckner's army and engaged Burnside's invading forces at Loudon, Tennessee.

At the Battle of Chickamauga Scott's Brigade was part of Gen. Pegram's Division and consisted of a detachment of John H. Morgan's Command, the First Louisiana Regiment, Second and Fifth Tennessee Cavalry Regiments and Robinson's Louisiana Battery. The Fifth Tennessee was part of the force detached from Forrest's Corps to participate in Gen. Joseph Wheeler's October 1863 raid into Sequachie Valley and Middle Tennessee and remained under Gen. Wheeler's command until the end of the war.

When Gen. Sherman engaged Gen. Joseph Johnston at Tunnel Hill in late April 1864, the Fifth Tennessee participated along with Ashby's, Baxter Smith's, James T. Wheeler's Regiments, and Major Akin's Ninth Tennessee Cavalry Battalion in a brigade commanded by Col. James T. Wheeler. With the Army of Tennessee from Dalton to Atlanta in 1864, the Fifth Tennessee Cavalry Regiment participated in the major engagements and was active especially in the Battle of New Hope Church and the fighting around Jonesborough and Lovejoy's Station. On June 30 Col. Henry M. Ashby was given command of the brigade and it was known from that time on as Ashby's Brigade.

After Sherman lay siege to Atlanta, the unit was part of Gen. Wheeler's raid on Federal supply lines from Dalton into East and Middle Tennessee.

At the time of Sherman's march to Savannah and on to North Carolina, the Fifth Cavalry Regiment was part of Wheeler's Cavalry, fought Federal Gen. Kilpatrick's Cavalry at Buck Head Church and at Waynesboro and skirmished frequently to harass and delay the Federal Army. The few who had survived the four years of war were present in the last major engagement at Bentonville and were paroled with Johnston's army in April 1865.

The following typescript of the First Regimental Order Book is based on a xerographic copy in the archives of the Rhea County Historical and Genealogical Society. The entries are carried forward from page to page over the handwritten pages and were obviously enscribed by several different persons. With the exception of a few very dim entries, the script is clear and only the orthography causes difficulty in reading. A final inserted sheet, not part of the document, dated March 1864 at Dalton, relates to a provision for retiring officers and is included here. There are mathematical calculations of no apparent consequence in some of the margins and the last sheet has random notes of a bond, a biblical quotation, and references to the politics of the 1860's. These have been omitted from the typescript.

The entries cover the period from February 1862 when the unit was First (Rogers') Regiment to February 28, 1863 after it had become Fifth (McKenzie's) Regiment. The entries are not in exact order either by date or order number, having been copied into the logbook somewhat randomly. Of the eighty entries only the last seven are headlined "5th Regt."

The Second Regimental Order Book (to be published later) covers the period from March 4, 1863 to April 2, 1865.

To facilitate reference, the orders are arranged here by order number or date; however, it should be noted that at least some of the orders entered under date of March 3, 1862 must have been issued at an earlier date and simply recorded on that date. The lack of internal evidence makes it impossible to establish exact dates. Too, for convenience, the orders are printed here with page breaks instead of running continuously from page to page.

This typescript copy has attempted to remain faithful to the original in spelling and punctuation, using bracketed comments only where it is deemed to be useful or essential for clarity. Footnote material is added for clarification and is from National Archive Service Records of the individual cavalrymen (abstracted in a separate document) unless a different source is cited.

The xerographic copies appended here are reduced to 77% of the original to accommodate this sheet size.

Carl E. Campbell
715 Brookfield Avenue
Chattanooga, TN 37412

January 7, 1997

CONTENTS

PART 1 — TYPESCRIPT OF ORDER BOOK

Orders of:
    1st Regiment Tennessee Cavalry 1
    2nd Regiment Tennessee Cavalry 64
    2nd Battalion Tennessee Cavalry 73
    5th Regiment Tennessee Cavalry 81
    Army of Tennessee 88
Organizational Summary 90
Summary of Orders 91
Index to Orders and Notes 93

PART 2 — COPIES OF ORIGINAL ORDERS 99

PART 1 — TYPESCRIPT OF ORDER BOOK

Headquarters
Knoxville Feby 5 1862[1]

Special Orders
    No. 19

(I) All officers are prohibited from granting furloughs. Furloughs already given are hereby revoked and all absentees are required to report to their proper officers for duty without delay.

(II) Requisitions for Subsistance cannot be approved unless accompanied by a morning report of the commands.

(III) Business will be transacted at Head quarters from 9 A.M. to 4 P.M. only.

D. Leadbetter[2]
Col., Commd'ng

---

[1] On February 5, 1862 Col. Leadbetter at Knoxville dispatched General Cooper, AIG at Richmond, "The cavalry, while expecting orders to join Gen. Crittenden has been directed to scour the counties of Scott, Morgan, and Campbell for the purpose of putting down rebellion, as well as to give prompt notice of any forward movement of the enemy." The 1st Regiment had engaged the enemy on February 3, a few miles north of Camp Schooler (*Official Records*, I-7, p. 118).

[2] Colonel Daniel Leadbetter, later Brigadier General, was sent to East Tennessee in November 1861 to maintain the railroads. On January 7, 1862 Col. Leadbetter dispatched Gen. Cooper, AIG at Richmond, that Gen. Carroll had left Knoxville and that he was in command there (*Official Records*, II-1, p. 869).

Head Quarters 1st Reg. Tenn. Cav.
Jacksborough, Tenn. 27 Feb. 1862

General Order No. 1[3]

There will be a detail of five men from each Company as Pickett Guards who will at eight Oclock move out on the various roads at least 3 miles from Town and remain on duty untill 6 Oclock A.M. They will then be relieved by a pickett of 3 men from each company who will remain on duty Scouting out for Four miles and remain on Duty untill relieved at 8 Oclock P.M.

Leut. Beeler[4] will act as officer of the guard to night, will visit the various post[s] at least twice through the night. Capt. McKenzie[5] will furnish the officer of the Day to morrow Who will take charge of the New guard and relieve Lieut. Beeler precisely at 6 o'clock A.M. Capt. Brocks[6] men will guard on the Maynardsville Road, Capt. Willets[7] the Mountain Road, Capt. Gorman[8] the Road to Cumberland Gap, Capt. Blackwell[9] Road to Clinton, Capt. McKenzie Road to Knoxville. The regular Stable guard in each company in addition to the above.

By order of
J. F. White, Leut Col
Commanding Battallion[10]
Montiaville Davenport, Adjt

---

[3] The Report of the 5th Regiment dated March 14, 1864 at Tunnel Hill stated "The Regiment was first organized at Knoxville January 7, 1862 and ordered at once to the Kentucky border to meet the army on its retreat from Fishing Creek." Apparently the staff had not kept the paperwork current.

[4] There is no record of a Lt. Beeler. Sgt. L. B. Beeler is shown as resigning on January 7, 1862 and Pvt. John Beeler is the only other Beeler listed in regimental records. (This and subsequent undocumented citations are drawn from the National Archive Service Records for the 5th (McKenzie's) Tennessee Cavalry Regiment.)

[5] Capt. George W. McKenzie, a Mexican War veteran, raised a Meigs County company (Company B, C in the 5th Regiment) which he commanded until promoted.

[6] Capt. A. J. Brock raised a Union County Company (Company A) which was mustered out on April 12, 1862 and was never part of the 5th Regiment.

[7] George W. Willett was First Lieutenant, Company H (B in the 5th Regiment). However, he signed the October-December and January-February muster rolls for the company as commander. He was dropped from the rolls on May 24, 1862.

[8] Capt. Thomas S. Gorman raised Company E (F in the 5th Regiment) in Cocke County. He was discharged on May 24, 1862, being over age at 48.

[9] J. L. Blackwell became captain and commander of Company F (A in the 5th Regiment) when Capt. White was promoted to Lieutenant Colonel.

[10] It is not clear why Lt. Col. White signed this order as commanding "Battalion" since it was issued from "Headquarters, 1st Reg. Tenn. Cav."

Head Quarters First Regt Tenn. Cav.
Jacksboro, Tenn. 28 Feb. 1862

Special Order No. 4[11]

In acordance with Millitary Law and the Army Regulations of the Confederate States. The offices vacated by promotion will be filled by promotion from the grades below. In Company F of the Regiment 1st Leut. J. L. Blackwell becomes the Capt., 2nd Leut. Wheeler[12] 1st Leut., Leut. Roberts[13] Second Leut., 1st Sargt G. C. White[14] Jun 2nd Leut., Second Sargent Reagon[15] 1st Sargent, 3rd Sarg't Alexander[16] 2nd Sarg't, 4th Sarg't Lowery[17] 3rd Sarg't, 1st Corporal Cannon[18] 4th Sargent, 2nd Corporal Jenkins 1st Corporal, 3 Corporal Huges[19] 2nd Corporal, 4th Corporal Taylor[20] 3 Corporal, and E. H. Cooksten[21] 4th Corporal. And these commissions to date from the 7th Jan. 1862.[22]

By Order of
Jno. F. Rodgers
Col., Comd Regt

---

[11] See Special Order 34, dated 9 March 1862, below.

[12] Lt. J. C. Wheeler died March 25, 1862.

[13] Lt. P. G. Roberts resigned March 5, 1862 because of "pulmonary consumption" and died in 1863.

[14] Lt. G. C. White was discharged May 24, 1862.

[15] A. J. Reagan became Captain of White's Company (A in the 5th Regiment) on December 17, 1862 and was paroled with the regiment on May 3, 1865.

[16] Sgt. S. H. Alexander was captured January 13, 1864 and was a prisoner at Camp Chase at war's end.

[17] Cpl. W. T. Lowry was discharged for blindness on September 1, 1862.

[18] Cpl. Robert Cannon died October 5, 1862 at Chickamauga, Tennessee.

[19] Cpl. Joshua Hughes was discharged September 17, 1862 being over age.

[20] Pvt. James Taylor, who deserted February 24, 1864, or Pvt. Jesse Taylor, who was AWOL after November 15, 1862.

[21] E. H. Croxton was later promoted to Lieutenant and resigned January 8, 1865 at Grahamville, South Carolina.

[22] As indicated in the note above, it appears that the regimental staff had been delayed in copying orders into the order book.

Headquarters
Jacksboro   Mar 1st /62

Jno. Jarnagin[23]

    Sir

You will deliver to Maj. Bridgeman's command[24] such commissary stores as he take with his command [sic] taking Receips for same.

Respt yours
Jno. F. Rodgers
Col. Cmmd

---

[23] Service Records for the regiment do not include John Jarnigan.

[24] Maj. John N. Bridgman was second in command of the 4th (Branner's) Tennessee Cavalry Battalion, also called the 1st, 2nd, and East Tennessee Cavalry Battalion. On May 24, 1862 this unit was consolidated with the 5th (McClellan's) Tennessee Cavalry Battalion to form the 2nd (Ashby's) Tennessee Cavalry Regiment with which the 5th (McKenzie's) Regiment was brigaded throughout most of the war.

Head Quarters 1st Reg Ten. Cav.
Jacksboro Mar 2 '62

Maj. Jno. M. Bridgeman
    Commander 4 Ten Battalion

        You will halt your command and fall back on Robertsvill or Montgomery, keeping out a Pickett force on the Jamestown road Leading from Knoxville to Montgomery. Report by Courier to the commander at Knoxville of any movements of the enemy. You will also communicate with Col. Vaughn[25] at Louden any information you get of the movements of the enemy. You will also report by courier to these Head Quarters.

                    Very Resp'y
                    Jno F. Rodgers
                    Cmd

---

[25] Col. John C. Vaughn, later Brigadier General, commanded the 3rd Tennessee Infantry Regiment which was returned from Virginia to East Tennessee in February 1862 at the request of Gov. Isham Harris to help suppress the Union sympathizers. The diaries of G. W. Clemmer and William E. Sloan (Tennessee State Archives) give details of the first year of this regiment.

Headquarters 1 Reg Tenn. Cav.
3 March 1862[26]

General Order
No. 2

The commanders of companys of this Regiment will parade their entire forces at 11 Oclock A.M. and make a close inspection of the arms belonging thereto and report to these Head Quarters.

By Order of
Jno. F. Rogers, Col.
M. Davenport, Agt.

---

[26] These several orders dated March 3, 1862 appear to have been issued at an earlier date and copied into the order book on March 3. Internal references make it illogical that they were first issued on March 3.

Headquarters 1st Reg. T. Cav.
Camp Skooler[27] 3rd Mar.[Feb.?] /62

Special Order No.

Capt. McKenzie will take up his line of march for Jacksboro, Ten. at 12 oclock Feb'y 4th 1862.[28] He will take with him Capt. Gorman's Com'y. After establishing the command judiciously at or near Jacksboro, he will proceed to reconnoiter the country in the direction of Williamsburg, Ky. and Chitwood Gap; if possible will immediately communicate with Knoxville giving any information he may get of the movements of the enemy. If any Superior force threatens his command he will fall back on the South side of the Clinch River, and destroy all the Boats, Canoes and Bridges on the River above Clinton. He will use great diligence to prevent a Surprise, Keeping a heavy Picket Guard Night and day.

By order of
J. F. White, Lt. Col.
Commdg

---

[27] Camp Schooler was located in Morgan County, apparently near Montgomery, the county seat at that time.

[28] On February 3, 1862 Lt. Col. White in Morgan County dispatched to Col. Leadbetter at Knoxville that he would "move McKenzie's and Gorman's companies, if possible, tomorrow on Jacksborough." (*Official Records*, I-7, p. 119).

Head Quarters 1st Regt Tenn. Cavalry
Jacksboro   March 3, 1862

Special Order No. 5

    Capt. G. M. Montgomery[29]

           Sir

              You will parade your company at 9 Oclock A.M. and proceed to the election of commissioned and non-comissioned officers of your company reporting the results to these Headquarters. If no choice is affected at the first balloting you will still continue until a choice is made.

                      By order of
                      J. F. Rogers, Col.
                M. Davenport, Adjutant

---

[29] Capt. John George Morgan Montgomery raised Company I (D in 5th Regiment) in Bradley County February 14, 1862. He later served the regiment as Lieutenant Colonel.

Headquarters 1 Reg. Ten. Cavalry
Jacksboro Ten. Mar 3, 1862

Special Order No. 6

James S. O'Neil, Company D[30]

Will proceed to Knoxville and procure supplies from the commanding Quarter master and ordinance stores for Regiment. Is hereby authorized to sign any and all receipts and make requisitions therefor and to do any and all lawful things and acts to enable him to procure coffee, candles, sugar, salt, flour, horse shoes, nails or iron, powder, shot cap, guns, saddles, bridles, printed blanks,[31] &c &c.

By order of
John F. Rogers, Col.
M. Davenport, Adjutant

---

[30] John S. O'Neal, AQM, was discharged late in 1862, being over age.

[31] Printed forms for record keeping.

Headquarters 1st Regt Ten. Cavalry
March 3, 1862

Special order No. 7

Jas. M. Martin[32] (of Company B)

Sir you are hereby detailed to act as commissary for the Regt until farther orders from these Head quarters.

By order of
Jno. F. Rogers, Col.

---

[32] James M. Martin was promoted January 20, 1862. He was last shown present on the July-August 1862 muster roll.

Head quarters 1st Regt Tenn. Cavalry
Jacksboro   March 3rd 1862

Special order No. 8

Robert S. Holt[33] of Company C

Is hereby detailed to assist Jas. M. Martin acting commissary for the Regiment untill farther orders from these Head quarters.

By order of
Jno. F. Rogers
Commanding Post

---

[33] Pvt. Robert S. Holt was discharged July 1, 1862 as over age.

						Head Quarters
					1st Regt Tenn. Cavalry
						Mar. 3, 1862

Special Order No. 9

      Jno. M. Bates[34] (of Company C)

                    Is hereby detailed to act as Quarter Master for this Regt until farther orders from these Head quarters.

						By order of
					Jno. F. Rogers, Col.

---

[34] Pvt. John M. Bates was transferred to 63rd Tennessee Infantry Regiment with Brown's Company on May 16, 1862.

Head Quarters
1st Regt Tenn. Cavalry Mar 3/62

Special order No. 10

    Fredrick Lindmen[35] (of Company D)

Is hereby detailed to act as assistant Quarter Master for the Regt untill farther orders from these Head quarters.

By order of
Jno. F. Rogers, Col.

---

[35] Pvt. Frederick E. Lindner was discharged November 12, 1862, being over age; a later note in his record states that he was not a Confederate citizen.

Head Quarters 1st Regt Tenn. Cavalry
March 3rd, 1862

Special Order No. 11

M. Davenport[36] (of Co. F)

Is hereby detailed to act as Adjutant for this Regt until farther orders from these Head quarters.

By order of
Jno. F. Rogers, Col.

---

[36] Monteville Davenport was made Adjutant January 7, 1862 and discharged as over age on May 1 or June 25 of that year, both dates being given in his service record.

Head Quarters 1st Regt Tenn. Cavalry
March 3rd 1862

Special Order No. 12

Edwin A. Broyles[37] (of Company G.)

Is hereby detailed to act as Sergt Major for this Regt until farther orders from these Head-quarters.

Jno. F. Rogers, Col.

---

[37] Edwin A. Broyles was made Sergeant Major on March 4, 1862.

Head Quarters 1st Regt. Tenn. Cavl'y

Special Order No. 13

R. A. McMahan,[38]

Acting Forriage Master

You will upon the arrival of trains of Forrage waggons report them to the public store house for unloading and deliver it out only upon the proper requisition.

Approved
by order of
Jno. F. Rogers, Col.
Comdg Post

---

[38] Pvt. R. A. McMahan was discharged by furnishing Joseph Edwards as a substitute on December 7, 1862.

Head Quarters 1st Regt Ten. Cavalry
March 3, 1862

Special Order No. 14

Dr. L. C. Moreland[39] (of Company F)

Is hereby detailed to act as asst Surgeon until farther order from these Head quarters.

By order of
Jno. F. Rogers, Col.

---

[39] The regimental records do not list Dr. Moreland.

                                               Head Quarters
                              1st Regt Tenn. Cavalry   Mar. 3/62

Special Order No. 15

        R. A. McMahan[40] (of Company B)

                        Is hereby detailed to act as
Forrage Master for this Regt until farther orders from these
Head quarters.

                                               By order of
                                          Jno. F. Rogers, Col.
                                                  Commdg Post

---
[40] See Special Order No. 13 above.

Head quarters 1st Regt Tenn. Cavalry
March 3, 1862

Special Order No. 16

Chas. McClary[41] (of Company "D")

Is hereby detailed to act as Waggon master for this Regt untill farther orders from these Head quarters.

By order of
Jno. F. Rogers, Col.

---

[41] Pvt. Charles M. McClary was last present for the March-April 1862 muster and later discharged as over age.

Head Quarters 1 Reg Tenn. Cav.
3 March 1862

Special Order No. 17

Dr. Geor. W. Ford[42]

        Cleveland

        Sir you are hereby appointed Surgeon of this Regiment untill farther orders from these head Quarters and will report yourself to the headquarters of this Reg immediately.

By order of
J. F. Rogers, Col.
Commanding Post

---

[42] The regimental records do not include Dr. Ford.

Head Quarters 1 Reg Tenn. Cavalry
Jacksboro Mar 4, 1862

Special Order No. 18

Lt. Geo. C. White,[43] Co (F)

Sir, you are hereby required to report yourself for duty to these Head quarters immeidately [sic], you will show this order to the commanding officer at Knoxville.

By order of
J. E. Wheeler 1st Lt.
Comm'g Company

{Approved by J. F. Rogers, Col.}
{   By J. F. White, Lt. Col.}

---

[43] Lt. George C. White was discharged May 24, 1862.

Head Quarters 1 Rg. Tn. Cav'y
Jacksboro Mar 4, 1862

Special order No. 19

The commanders of Companies A, B, & G[44] will parade their men at Head quarters precisely at 11 oclock today, and report to Maj. McLin for head [sic] marching orders, taking their entire camp equipage with them.

By order of
J. F. Rogers, Col.
M. D. Davenport, Adjt.

---

[44] Companies A, B, and G were the companies raised by Brock, McKenzie, and McLin. McKenzie's and McLin's companies became Companies C and H in the 5th Regiment. Brock's company was mustered out on April 12, 1862 and never served as part of the 5th Regiment.

Head Quarters 1st Regt Ten. Cavalry
Jacksboro Mar 4, 1862

Special Order No. 20

Capt. A. J. Brock will make a requisition for 20,000 G. D.[45] caps, 100 lb rifle powder, Buck shot and Lead, and for'd to these Head Quarters immediately.

By order of
Jno. F. Rogers
Com'g

---

[45] Percussion caps.

Head Quarters 1st Regt Ten. Cav'y
March 5th 1862

Special Order No. 21

The commander of Company "F"[46] will furnish Twenty-five effective men at 8½ O'clock to be placed under Comm'd of Lt. Col. White.

By order of
Jno. F. Rogers, Col.
M. Davenport, Ajt.

---

[46] Company F (A in the 5th Regiment) was raised by John F. White.

Head Quarters 1st Regt T. Cav'y
March 5, 1862

Special order
No. 22

The commander of Com'y "C"[47] will furnish Forty men at 8½ Oclock today to be placed under comm'd of Lt. Col. White.

By order of
Jno. F. Rogers, Col.
M. Davenport, Ajt.

---

[47] Company C (Brown's Company) was transferred to infantry May 16, 1862.

Head Quarters 1st Reg T. Cav'y
March 3, 1862

Special order No. 23

The commander of Com'y "E"[18] will furnish twenty men at 8½ Oclock A.M. to be placed under com'd of Lt. Col. White.

By order of
Jno. F. Rogers, Col.
M. Davenport, Ajt.

---

[18] Company E (F in the 5th Regiment) was raised by Thomas S. Gorman.

March 3rd, 1862

Special Order No. 24

The comm'dr of comp'y "D"[49] will furnish thirty men to be placed under com'd of Lt. Col. White today at 8½ Oclock.

By order of
Jno. F. Rogers, Col.
M. Davenport, Ajt.

---

[49] Company D (E in the 5th Regiment) was raised by Robert W. McClary.

Head Quarters   1st Reg T. Cavalry
Jacksboro,   Mar 3

Special Ordr No 25

The pickets at Big Creek Gap will pass Mr. Graham & Rogers[50] through their lines unmolested.

By order of
Jno. F. Rogers, Col.[51]

---

[50] Messrs Graham and Rogers have not been identified.

[51] This is the last order issued by Col. Rogers. W. G. Allen, in unpublished reminiscences, wrote that Col. Rogers became ill and was removed to Cleveland, Tennessee, where he died.

Head Quarters 1st Regt Ten. Cav'y
Jacksboro, March 6, 1862

Gen'l Order No. 3

The Comm'g officers of the respective companies belonging to this Regt are hereby required to make out a detail for Pickets the night before, and see that they report themselves at these Head Quarters precisely at 6 Oclock A.M.

By order of
J. F. White Lt. Col., Cmd
M. Davenport, Ajt.

                                    Head Quarters 1 Reg Ten. Cav.
                             6th March 186..   Jacksborough 1862

General Order
      No. 4

    Commanders of companies are hereby commanded [to] use
their best endeavors to have the sabres sharpened at the
earliest opportunity, detailing a suitable non-commissioned
officer to superintend it in each company

                                            By order of
                                  Lieut. Col. J. F. White
                                       M. Davenport, Ajt.

Head Quarters 1st Regt Ten. Cavalry
Jacksboro Mar 6, 1862

Special Order No. 26

Capt. Brown & Lieut. Coxey[52] will put their companys in marching order precisely at 8½ Oclock tommorrow morning. Each will apply to Qtr Master for transportation for company equipage, and for 25 axes for ea company and 100 lbs Blasting Powder.[53] The officers will apply at Head quarters at 2 Oclock P.M. today for instructions.

By order of
J. F. White, Lieut. Col.
M. Davenport, Ajt.

---

[52] Lt. John B. Coxsey was in command of McClary's Company at this time.

[53] The narrow mountain passes were sometimes blocked against the enemy by blasting rocks into the roads.

Head Quarters 1st Regt T. Cav'y
Jacksboro Mar 6, 1862

Special Order No. 27

The comm'drs of companies "E," "F," & "I"[54] will furnish thirty-five men in the morning to be distributed as follows: Co "E" Eight, Co. "F" Seventeen and Co. "I" Ten, all of which will be required to be ready to march precisely at 8½ Oclock A.M.

By order of
J. F. White, Lt. Col. Cmdg
M. Davenport, Ajt.

---

[54] Company I was J. G. M. Montgomery's Bradley County Company (D in the 5th Regiment).

Head Quarters 1st Regt T. Cav'ry
Mar 7th 1862

Sp. Ordr No. 28

    The comm'drs of Companies C & D will put their comp's in marching order precisely at 1 oclock P.M. instead of 8½ oclock A.M. as previsely or'd.

By order of
J. F. White, Lt. Col., Com'g
M. Davenport, Ajt.

Head Quarters 1st Rgt Ten. Cav.
Jacksboro, Mar 8th 1862

Spl order No. 29

Capt. W. L. Brown has leave of absence from camps and is relieved of camp duties until the 18th[55] inst at which time he will report himself at Regimental Head quarters for duty.

By order of
J. F. White
Lt. Col. Commdg

---

[55] Capt. Brown was with the regiment on March 13. See Special Order No. 38 below.

Head Quarters 1st Reg. T. Cav'y
Jacksboro Mar 8th 1862

Special Order No. 30

Capt. Jno. Bates,[56] Act'g Regimental Qt master

Sir, you are hereby authorized to hire a sufficient no. of waggons to haul hay and corn for the regt in addition to Gov't teams now under your control and may bind the Government to pay the following prices: that is to say for a

(Per day)	Two horse team and waggon	3.00
"	Three " " " "	3.50
"	Four " " " "	4.00

with 50c per day to the driver of the team. If you cannot hire teams at these prices you are authorized and required to press them wherever you can find them using discretion in the exercise of the duty. You will pay the owners of pressed teams in accordance with the above tariff of prices.

By order of
J. F. White, Lieut. Col.
M. Davenport, Ajt.

---

[56] John M. Bates ranked as Private.

Head Quarters 1st Reg T. Cav.
Jacksboro, Mar 9 1862

Spl order No. 31

Thomas M. Hoyl[57] is detailed as bearer of dispatches to Knoxville.

By order of
J. F. White, Lt. Col.
Comdg.
M. Davenport, Adjt.

---

[57] Lt. Thomas M. Hoyl was taken prisoner on March 14, 1862 at Big Creek Gap along with Lt. Col. White. He was exchanged on September 16 at Vicksburg. He later served with the 63rd Tennessee Infantry and with Lillard's 3rd Tennessee Infantry.

                                    Head Quarters 1 Regiment Ten. Cav.
                                                       9 March 1862

Special Order 32

Lieut. J. C. Wheler[58]

         Commanding Company (F)

                        Sir you will take steps to
put your company under marching orders.

                                              By order of
                                         J. F. White, Lt. Col.

---
[58] See Note 12.

Head Quarters 1 Reg. Ten. Cav
9 March 1862

Special Order No. 33}

Mr. Bruce

Information having been received at these Head Quarters that you are selling Whiskey to soldiers belonging to this command I hereby notify you that if you sell or give any more liquors to these men I will cause you to be brought to this place and inflict upon you the severest punishment of Law for such offences.

J. F. White
Lt. Col. Commanding

Head Quarters 1st Reg Tennessee
Jacksborough 9 March 1862

Special Order No. 34[59]

In accordance with the Regulations of the Army of the Confederate States the vacancy occasioned in commissioned officers by the resignation of Lieut. P. G. Roberts[60] will be filled by regular promotion from the officers below. First sargent A. J. Reagan[61] will become 2 Lieut, Lieut Jun. 2 Sarg Alexander[62] 1st sargent, 3 sargent Lowery[63] 2nd sargent, 4 sargent Cannon[64] 3 sargent, 1 corporal 4 sargent, 2 corp Hughs[65] 1 corp, 3 corporal Taylor[66] 2 corporal, 4th Corporal Croxten[67] 3rd Corporal, and Private Wm. H. Hale[68] is promoted and appointed 4th Corporal.

By order of
J. F. White, Lt. Col.
Commanding Regt

---

[59] See Special Order No. 4, dated 28 February 1862, above.

[60] See Note 13.

[61] See Note 15.

[62] See Note 16.

[63] See Note 17.

[64] See Note 18.

[65] See Note 19.

[66] Pvt. James Taylor deserted February 24, 1864 and took oath as rebel deserter at Chattanooga on February 26, 1864.

[67] See Note 21.

[68] Pvt. W. F. Hale deserted November 30, 1863.

Proceedings of a general court martial convened at Jacksboro, by virtue of the following order:

Headquarters 1st Rgt Tn. Cav'y
Jacksboro, Mar 9th 1862

Gen'l Order No. 5

A general court martial will assemble at the Court House at 12 Oclock M on the 9th Inst for the trial of James & Wm. Dobins[69] and such others as may be brought before it.

Detail for the Court

Capt. Montgomery 1st Reg T. Cavalry Co "I," Pres't of the court.

Lieut	J. C. Wheeler	Co	"F"
"	John Baker	"	"E"
"	F. P. Sloan	"	"I"

Lieut. R. F. Sloan of comp'y "I" is appointed Judge advocate of the court.

By comm'd of J. F. White
Lieut. Col.

Charges against James Dobins -

First for becoming intoxicated while on Picket duty, 2nd for leaving his Post while on Said duty without permission from anyone having power to relieve him and thereby leaving the Post unguarded.

James Dobins pleads not guilty.

Testimony of G. H. Blancet,[70] private in Co. "F" questioned by Judge advocate, -

Did you see James Dobins on the 8th March intoxicated?
    Answer, Yes.

Was he on Picket duty?
    Ans. Yes.

Did you see him at the still house?
    Ans. No.

---

[69] Pvt. James Dobbins, after lengthy absence without leave, was detained in East Tennessee by Gen. Humes. Pvt. William Dobbins was present at every recorded muster and surrendered with the regiment in April 1865.

[70] Pvt. G. H. Blancet was killed July 15, 1862 at Wallace's Cross Roads.

Did he state to you where he got his liquor?
    Ans. At the Still-house.

Where was he on Picket?
    Ans. At the forks of the road.

How far is the Still-house from the Post?
    Ans. About 1 mile.

Was he relieved by any one before he left?
    Ans. No.

Did he leave the Post before relieved?
    Ans. Yes.

Cross questioned by Ajt. Davenport:

Was you Sergt that day?
    Ans. Yes.

Were you not ordered to Scout the road that day?
    Ans. Yes.

Were you ordered to ride toward town?
    Ans. Yes.

Did you order him to Scout the road towards the Still-house?
    Ans. Yes.

Did you consider him off of his post when at the Still House?
    Ans. No.

Re-examined by Judge advocate:

Was the Still-House on the road?
    Ans. Yes.

Re-examined by Ajt Davenport:

Do you know where Dobins got the whiskey?
    Ans. No.

                                              his
                                     G. H. X Blancet
                                            mark

Testimony of Rob't Cannon.[71]

Questioned by Judge advocate -

Were you on Picket duty with James Dobins?
    Ans. No.

Did you see him intoxicated yesterday?
    Ans. I supposed he was.

Where were you when you met him?
    Ans. About 1 mile from town.

Did you have any conversation with him?
    Ans. No.

                                        R. M. Cannon

Testimony of Elis Philips[72], private in Co. "F."

Questioned by Judge advocate.

Were you out on Picket with James Dobins yesterday?
    Ans. No.

Did you see Mr. Dobins yesterday evening?
    Ans. Yes, after dark.

Was he intoxicated when you saw him?
    Ans. I do not know.

---

[71] See Note 18.

[72] Pvt. Ellis Phillips left camp without permission about November 10, 1862 and joined the 3rd Confederate Cavalry.

Testimony of Tol Cruce,[73] private in comp. "F."

Questioned by Judge advocate.

Did you see James Dobins yesterday?
    Ans. Yes.

Where was he?
    Ans. On his line of duty.

Were you on picket duty with him?
    Ans. Yes.

Where did he get his whiskey?
    Ans. At the still house.

Cross examined by Adjt. Davenport.

Was the Still House close to the road where you were ordered to Scout?
    Ans. Yes at the end of the line.

                        Toliver Crews

Testimony of J. G. Davenport,[74] private in Co. "F."

Questioned by Judge Advocate.

Did you see James Dobins yesterday evening?
    Ans. Yes.

Was he intoxicated?
    Ans. I do not know.

Testimony of W. F. Hale[75] in Com "F"

Questioned by Judge Advocate,

Did you see James Dobins yesterday?
    Ans. Yes.

Was he intoxicated?
    Ans. I do not know.

---

[73] Pvt. Tolliver Crews, was discharged in November 1862 as under age at 16.

[74] Pvt. J. G. Davenport transferred to Malone's 9th Alabama Cavalry late in 1862.

[75] See Note 68.

Testimony of Sims Benton,[76] private in Co. "F."

Questioned by Judge Advocate,

Did you see James Dobins yesterday evening?
    Ans. Yes.

Was he intoxicated?
    Ans. I do not know. I never spoke to him.

    Verdict of the court is guilty of the 1st Charge. The penalty that he stand on extra duty alternately for three nights.

                          J. G. M. Montgomery, Capt.,
                        Lieut R. F. Sloan, Judge Ad'e.
                                  in 1 Regt Ten. Cavalry.

                                          Approved
                              J. F. White, Lt. Col.
                              and Pres't of C. M.

Charges against Wm. Dobins.

1st for becoming intoxicated while on Picket duty. 2nd Leaving his post without any authority from any officer having charge of the Post and 3rd for intercepting the property of citizens and otherwise conducting himself in a maner predudicial [sic] to the good order and discipline of the army of the C. S. A.

    Wm. Dobins pleads not guilty.

Testimony of G. H. Blancet, private in co "F."

Questioned by Judge Advocate,

Did you see Wm. Dobins on Picket line on yesterday evening?
    Ans. Yes.

Was he intoxicated?
    Ans. Yes.

---

[76] Pvt. Little Page Sims Benton deserted February 1, 1864.

Where was he at that time?
    Ans. At Sharp's on the Clinton road.

Was he on Picket duty?
    Ans. Yes.

Did he leave his line of duty?
    Ans. No.

Did he intercept the person or property of any individual?
    Ans. No.

Was he conducting himself in a quiet manner?
    Ans. No.

How was he conducting himself?
    Ans. He was laughing and talking to the other boys.

                                his
                          G. H. X Blancet
                                mark

Testimony of Toliver Crews, private in Co. "F."

Questioned by Judge Advocate.

Were you on Picket yesterday with Wm. Dobins?
    Ans. Yes.

Was he intoxicated.
    Ans. Yes.

Was he off his line of Picket duty?
    Ans. No.

What was he doing while intoxicated?
    Ans. He was walking about laughing and talking.

Did you see him disturbing any private property belonging to citizens?
    Ans. No.

Was he conducting himself predudicial to good order?
Ans. He was not.

          Toliver Crews

Verdict of the Court.

Guilty of the 1st charge.
The penalty that he stand an extra duty alternately for three nights.

          J. G. M. Montgomery
          Lieut. R. F. Sloan

          Capt. 1st Reg. Cav'y
   Judge Advocate and Pres't of the court

            Approved
       J. F. White, Lieut.Col.
            Commdg.

Head Quarters 1st R. T. Cav.
Jacksboro, Mar 11, 1862

Spl ordr No. 35

2nd Lieut. Sloan,[77] Co. "I" will take a detachment of 15 men and Scout on the mountain and Huntsville road observing closely for evidence of the presence of the enemy or his pickets. He will report at Head Quarters on his return.

By order of
J. F. White, Lt. Col.
M. Davenport, Adjt.

---

[77] Lt. Felix P. or Lt. Robert F. Sloan.

[*The following entry is lined out*]

> Head Quarters 1st R. T. Cav
> Mar 11th 1862

Lieut. J. C. Wheeler has leave of absence from company and is relieved of camp duties until the 22nd Inst. at the expiration of which time he will report himself at Head Quarters for duty.

> J. F. White, Lieut. Col.

Headquarters, 1 Reg Ten. Cavalry
11 March 1862

Lieut. James Wheler has leave of absence from camp and is relieved from camp duties till the 26th of month at which time he will report to Regt. Head Quarters for Duty.

J. F. White
Lt. Col.

Head Quarters 1 Reg Ten. Cav.
Jacksborough 11 March /62

Special Order No. 36

Commanding Officer Company (F)[78]

        Will on the arrival of the provision train from Knoxville make requisition & draw 5 days additional Rations, will apply to Quartermaster for transportation camp [?] and equippage and as soon thereafter as possible will move to such point on the Clinch River as will best enable him to cover all of the various crossings of the same. He will arrest all renegades from East Tenn who are enroute for Ky. disarming them and send the Ring leaders to Knoxville, will Scout daily in all directions reporting by courier to these Head Quarters.

By order of
J. F. White, Lt. Col.
Commanding

---

[78] Lt. John Baker of this company signed an ordnance requisition on March 11, 1862.

Head Quarters 1st R T Cav.
Jacksboro, Mar 11th 1862

Special Order No. 37

Philo Shepherd[79] is hereby appointed Regimental Steward for First Regt Tenn Cavalry. He will at once enter upon the duties of his office, reporting to the Surgeon for duty.

By order of
J. F. White, Lieut. Col.
M. Davenport, Adjt.

---

[79] The regimental records do not include Philo Shepherd.

Head Quarters 1st Reg. Ten. Cav
Mar 12th 1862

Gen'l Order No. 6

In obedience to instructions and orders rec'd from Head Quarters there will be no men furloughed from camps only upon Surgeons certificate of disability.

By order of
J. F. White, Lieut. Col.
Commdg

Head Qtrs 1st Reg T. Cavalry
Jacksboro, Mar 13 1862

Special Order No. 38[80]

Capt. Brown, Lieut. Al Kinson[81] & Lieut. Brittain[82] are hereby appointed as a board of Survey, to value the horses belonging to the company of Capt. A. J. Brock, in the 1st Regt Ten. Cavalry.

By order of
J. F. White, Lt. Col.
M. Davenport, Ajt.

---

[80] A few days later on March 26 Gen. Leadbetter at Kingston was ordered to, "Inspect the [cavalry] companies under your command, especially the First Regiment East Tennessee Cavalry, and report to headquarters...." He was further ordered to recommend if any should be disbanded (*Official Records*, I-10-2, p. 366). On April 12 Brock's Company was mustered out of service.

[81] Pvt. A. J. Kinser (or Kincer) was wounded by the enemy in Scott County April 1, 1862 and unable for service thereafter.

[82] Benjamin F. Britten (or Brittain) transferred with Brown's Company to the 63rd Tennessee Infantry Regiment and was elected as Captain of Company H in that regiment on May 16, 1862.

March 13th 1862

Spl Ordr No. 39

Lieut. Baker[83] of Co "E", Lieut. R. F. Sloan and Lieut F. P. Sloan both of Co. "I" will meet immediately in committee to examine certain bacon bought by the Quartermaster which was issued to certain companies, and returned, and report to these Headquarters.[84]

By order of
J. F. White,[85] Lieut. Col.

Jacksboro Tenn.
March 13, 1862

We the undersigned committee of the 1st Rgt Tenn. Cavalry having made the necessary examination find 73½ lb of bacon that is unfit for use in the commissary department.

Lieut. R. F. Sloan, Co "I"
"   F. P. Sloan   "   "
"   John Baker   "   E

---

[83] Lt. John Baker was discharged May 24, 1862, being over age.

[84] On February 19, Gen. Cooper at Richmond had dispatched Col. Leadbetter at Knoxville that an agent had been sent to "attend to the matter of bacon."

[85] This is the last order issued by Lt. Col. White. On March 14 at 6:00 A.M. the 49th Indiana Volunteers commanded by Col. James P. T. Carter surprised McClary's and Brown's Companies at Big Creek Gap, taking Lt. Col. White and Lt. Thomas M. Hoyl prisoner and killing, wounding, and capturing several men. Gen. Kirby Smith felt the capture was "the result of treachery." (*Official Records*, I-10-1, p. 19). The Governor of Ohio immediately requested a pardon for Lt. Col. White, but he was never returned to duty.

Head Quarters 1st Regt Ten Cav'y
Jacksboro March /1862

Spl Ordr No. 40

Lieut McMahan[86] will take a detail of 8 men from Comp. "E" and the comd'r of Comp. I will detail 7 men to go with him. Start at 15 minutes after 2 Oclock P.M. and Scout the Huntsville Road 2 or three miles out beyond the top of the mountain.

By order of
Capt. J. G. M. Montgomery
Comm'er of Post

---

[86] Lt. McKinney McMahan was discharged May 24, 1862, being over age.

Hd Qtrs Kingston,[87] Tenn.
May 31st 1862

Gen'l Order   }
   No.   }

   John L. ONeal[88], Will act as Qtr Master for the 1st Reg Ten. Cav. and the various officers non-com'd off. & privates of that command and the post Qtr Master will give him the respect and obedience becoming his position.

             Jno. B. McLin, Major
               Comdg Post

---

[87] On March 23, 1862 H. L. Clay, AIG at Knoville, had dispatched Gen. Leadbetter to "proceed with as much dispatch as possible with the remainder of your brigade to Kingston. It is all important that the advances to Kingston from Montgomery and Crossville shall be carefully observed." (*Official Records*, I-10-2, p. 356).

[88] See Note 30.

Hd Qtrs Kingston Tenn.
June the 8th 1862

Special Order }[89]
No.   }

    The commanders of companies now with their companies with energy and decision will see that each man of his Company cleans up and see that his gun is in the best shooting condition in which he can place it, that his saber belt &C. is at hand; that each man is provided with ten rounds of amunition, haver sack, ball pouch, powder flask, bridle, saddle blanket and all a soldiers accouterments be placed each man's to its self so that in few minutes they will be ready to obey any order to scout, fight or whatnot without being in one another's way and without confusion.

    This Order must be obeyed.

Most Respectfully
John B. McLin, Col.
Commanding Post

---

[89] On June 4 and again on June 6 Col. McLin, commanding at Kingston, was ordered to be vigilant since it was expected that the enemy would move toward Montgomery and Kingston (*Official Records*, I-10-2, pp. 585, 592).

Hd Qtrs Kingston, Ten.
June 9th 1862

Gen'l Order }
No.   }

    Commanders of companies of this Regt will have their tents stacked and stored in some suitable and safe place under direction of the Qtr Master of this Regt except one tent and 2 flies for a company. And be ready to move the whole company by 9 o'clock A.M. tomorrow, taking with them their amunition, said tent & flies to the Co. and all their camp equipage. They will move to the left of the Battalion of the Geo. Cav. [Georgia Cavalry] near center of inf. [infantry] and take up their encampment.

    [Page torn and remainder missing]

                              Hd Qtrs 1st Regt Tenn. Caval.
              Camp Allston[90] near Kingston, June 18th 1862

Order No. }
          }

          Commanders of companies will see that
there is no horse racing by their men. Any violation of this
order Commanders of Companies will immediately arrest the
parties and bring them to these Hd Qtrs or they themselves
will be held responcible.

                                          By Order of
                                    Lt. Col. Comdg Regt
                               E. A. Broyles, Acting Adjt.

---

[90] Named for Benjamin Allston, brigade commander, who died from wounds.

                                    Hd Qtrs 1st Regt Tenn. Cav.
                                    Camp Allston, June 22nd 1862[91]

Orders No. }
           }

       All officers and Soldiers belonging to this regt are hereby prohibited from --?-- [bathing?] in the river at or near the spring or watering place.

                                              By Order of
                                    Lt. Col. G. W. McKenzie
                                              Commdr Regt
                                    E. A. Broyles, Acting Adjt

---

[91] On June 22 J. B. Belton, AAG at Knoxville, dispatched to Lt. Col. McLin at Lloyd's Crossroads, "The major general commanding has received no report from you. He directs that you will inform him immediately how your command is employed...." And again on June 23, "No reports of your movements have yet been received..." On June 24, Gen. Kirby Smith, in a dispatch to Gen. Stevenson asked, "Where is Major McLin's cavalry?" (*Official Records*, I-16-2, pp. 699, 703-704).

                                        Hd Qtrs 1st Regt Tenn. Cavalry
                                        Camp Allston, Kingston, Tenn.
                                                    July 1st 1862

Orders }[92]
No.   }

The Commanders of each Company of the companies of this Regt at this place will have their companies with all their cooking utensils, one tent and two files [flies] to each Company and six days unprepared rations all packed and in their wagons (which will be furnished by the Qtr Master.) Horses saddled and ready to mount and march by 10 Oclock A.M. The Commander of each Company will be expected to see that every man of his company march not only in column but in regular order and promptly closed up. Ten oclock not eleven is must in this order.

                                                    By Order of
                                                Jno. B. McLin, Col.
                                                    Comdg Regt
                                                    R. F. Sloan[93]
                                                    Acting Adjutant

---

[92] On June 30, H. H. Clay, AAG at Knoxville dispatched Col. McLin at Wallace's Cross Roads, "...The general directs that you push out scouts as far as possible into the valley ..." (*Official Records*, I-16-2, p. 714). A report from Company C states, "Left Kingston July 1 and marched to Maynardsville, scouted the country toward Taswell and Cumberland Gap."

[93] Lt. Robert F. Sloan served as adjutant until he was wounded by a runaway horse. His brother, William, described the circumstances in his diary.

Hd Qrs 1st Regt Tenn. Cavalry
Camp Near Maynardsville Tenn.
July 4th 1862

Special Order }
No.   }

    At Seven Oclock A.M. tomorrow the commanders of the companies of this Regt will each be ready to move with his entire company and at the command of a Regimental officer will form, be thrown into regular column and march compact across the creek to our newly selected camping ground in the woods.

    The companies will be encamped in correct line in the order of their letters, Company "B" on the right.

    Each company will dig sinks front of the center of their encampment which must be the place of private resort for the men that our beautiful and shady woods be not made filthy past enjoyment. There will be sinks dug in rear for the use of the field and staff officers.

    Reveille Roll call will be sounded at day break twenty minutes after which the 1st sergent of the companies under directions of commissioned officers without one moments delay will commence calling the roll marking the absentees. Immediately thereafter stable call will be sounded when the commanders of companies will see that the companies proceed immeadiately to water, feed, curry, and rub their horses thoroughly under the supervision of a Sergent of the Company who will see that the men move off regularly to and from water and keep properly closed. The N C officers having charge of squads will see that all the horses of their squad are watered at that time if possible. One man can ride a horse and lead three if members of the squad are absent or incapable of taking care of their horse.

    Surgeon's calls will be sounded at 5½ Oclock A.M. when the sick will be conducted by the 1st sergents of the companies to the Surgeons Quarters.

    Drill call will be sounded at 6 Oclock A.M. when the commanders of companies will see that all their men present for duty turn out dismounted, none will be excused from drill except those excused by the surgeon. Dismounted drill from 6 to 8 Oclock. Officer's call will be sounded at 9 Oclock A.M. when all the officers will assemble at Regt Hd Qrs for drill and instruction for two hours. Water call will be sounded at 10 Oclock A.M. Drill call for N. C. officers will be sounded at 2 Oclcok P.M. when all N. C. officers not on other duty will be assembled at Regimental Hd Qrs and be instructed and drilled under the directions and supervision of the Comdg officer of the Regt. N. C. officers drill from 2 to 4 Oclock P.M. Water call will be sounded at 2 Oclock P.M. Drill call will be sounded at 4 Oclock P.M. when companies will turn out mounted. Stable call will be sounded at 6 Oclock P.M. Dress parade at sundown. Tattoo roll call will be sounded at 8½ Oclock P.M. Taps at 9 Oclock when all lights will be extinguished and all noise and confusion in camps surpressed.

I. Not more than five men from each company will be allowed to be absent from camps at once. They to have a permit signed by the commanding officer of the Company and counter signed by the adjutant of the Regiment.

II. Call for guard mounting will be sounded at 8 Oclock A.M. when the details for guard will be conducted to the Regimental parade ground by the 1st Sergents of companies. Horses may be watered opposite the front of the encampment in the nearest branch but never higher up the branch which must be kept clean for culinary purposes.

For each of the foregoing calls except reveille there must be immediate complyance.

There will be company inspection of arms (guns & sabers) by company commanders every sabeth morning and both are expected to be kept bright and in as good repair as practable. All guns that have not been recently inspected will have the loads drawn from them immediately and the guns cleaned out thoroughly and put in good fix. All guns from which the load cannot be drawn will be brought and reported to Hd Qrs.

Commanders of companies will have opened in front of their encampments broad and convenient passways to water so if need be one man can ride a horse and lead three. In connection with each company encampment there will be cleaned up and handsomely placed a company parade ground.

The commanders of companies and their assistants will be expected to see that the N. C. officers having charge of Squads have the arms and equipments of each man kept separate and separate from those of the other men for the purpose of securing order and prompedness [sic].

Most Respectfully
Jno B. McLin, Col.
Comdg Regt

Hd Qrs 2nd Regt Tenn. Cavl.[94]
Camp Maynardsville, Tenn.
July 12, 1862

Special Order }
No.   }

        Private[95] in Comp. "K" of this Regt is hereby appointed forage master for the same and all his legitimate and lawful orders and acts connected with the same shall be respected as the same.

By order of
Jno. B. McLin, Col.
Comdg Regt

---

[94] This is the first order issued under the heading "2nd Regiment Tennessee Cavalry."

[95] The individual's name is omitted from this order. The service record for John W. C. (Coffee) Williamson, Company D (E in 5th Regt) states that he was detailed as forage sergeant on July 9, 1862 by Maj. McLin.

Hd Qrs 2nd Regt Tenn. Cav'l
Maynardsville, July 18th 1862

Lt. Col. McKenzie

Will go immediately and discover where the four companies of this Regt recently stationed at Walleses X roads[96] Cos "E," "F," "G," & "K" now are, take command of the same, conduct them back to Walles X Roads and guard and defend that pass, discover the advance of any enemy from the mountains into Powles Valley, all along the space between Walles X Roads and Fincastle inclusive and report to these Hd Qrs immiadeately [sic] and to Dept Hd Qrs Knoxville. All the orders heretofore issued to Capt. Blackwell and Mims will be faithfully obeyed, all that may be of importance to the publick service.

Lt. Col. Carter[97] with his command will shortly relieve Lt. Col. McKenzie and the companies above alluded to shortly at which time Lt. Col. McKenzie and his command will promptly move to Munster's ford of Clinch and report to Col. Ashby[98] for orders.

Most Respectfully
Jno. B. McLin, Col.
Comdg Regt

---

[96] On July 15, 1862 H. L. Clay, AAG at Knoxville, dispatched to Gen. C. L. Stevenson at Bean's Station: "Our cavalry at Wallace's Cross Roads (four companies) under the command of Capt. Mims (Col. McLin's Second Tennessee Cavalry) was surprised by the enemy at 11 o'clock this morning. Capt. Mims reports from Mynatt's Cross Roads that no scouts had been ordered out today and when his pickets were driven in he advanced to meet, as he supposed, a small force, when he discovered two full regiments advancing on his flank. He retreated with the loss of about 20 men (captured, killed and wounded), all his baggage &c." (*Official Records*, I-16-1, p. 812).

[97] Lt. Col. James E. Carter, commanding 14th (Carter's) Tennessee Cavalry Battalion.

[98] Col. Henry M. Ashby, commanding 2nd (Ashby's) Tennessee Cavalry Regiment, later brigade commander.

                                    Hd Qrs 2nd Regt Tenn. Cav.
                                        Maynardsville Tenn.
                                            July 18, 1862

Special Order }
No.   }

    Capt. Mims will report immediately to Major Clay, A. A. G. at Knoxville.[99]

                                            By order of
                                        Jno. B. McLin, Col.
                                            Comdg Regt

---

[99] His service record states that Capt. Mims was in suspension or arrest at Knoxville by order of Col. Allston.

Hd Qrs 2nd Regt Tenn. Cavl.
Maynardsville, Tenn, July 20 /62

Special Order }
No.   ]

    Capt. W. O. Martin[100] will take command of his whole company that are capable of service, officers and privates with one day's prepared rations and be ready to march with blankets precisely at 8 Oclock P.M. which captain will report to these Hd Qrs for further instructions.

By command of
Col. J. B. McLin
Comdg Regt

---

[100] Lt. W. O. Martin was promoted to Captain on May 24, 1862. He was ordered dropped from the rolls by the Secretary of War on March 1, 1864, apparently for being absent without leave.

Hd Qrs 2nd Regt Tenn Cavl.
Maynardsville, Tenn. July 20 /62

The commanders of each of the comp's will report to these Hd Qrs the exact number of men able for duty in case of emergency who are not on the scout that has just returned or on picket last night.

By order of
Col. Jno B. McLin
Comdg Regt
R. F. Sloan, A.A.

Hd Qrs 2nd Regt Tenn. Cav.
Maynardsville, July 20 /62

Special Order }
No.   }

    Z. L. Ragon[101] who has been acting as Sergent in Com. "B" of said Regt because of his inefficiency and gross neglect of duty in office is hereby reduced to the rank of a private and J. D. Blevins[102] of s. com. [said company] is hereby appointed Sergent in s. comp. and all his acts and orders in this connexion are required to be respected and obeyed. This order will be read to the com. at roll call.

                                                J. B. McLin, Col.
                                                  Comdg Regt

---

[101] Pvt. Z. H. Reagan was present on the March 11, 1864 muster roll but there are no further references.

[102] James D. Blevins, later Lieutenant, was in command of the company when the regiment surrendered in April 1865.

Hd Qrs 2nd Regt Tenn. Cavl.
Maynardsville, Tenn, July 22 /62

Special Order }
No.   ]

Robert L. Williams[103] Second Corporal in Comp. B because of his rebellious and disorderly conduct in refusing to act as corporal of the guard when detailed for the duty and insultingly and disrespectfully asserting he would not do so and for cursing and treating with great disrespect the orderly sergent detailing him for that duty is hereby forbidden from this time forth to act as corporal in s. com. but is hereby reduced to the position of private and York M. King[104] is hereby appointed to this office of 2nd corporal in Sd. Com. and all his legitimate acts and orders in connection therewith are required to be respected and obeyed as such.

By order
J. B. McLin, Col.
Comdg Regt

---

[103] Pvt. Robert L. Williams was with the regiment at its surrender in April 1865 as a paroled prisoner.

[104] Regimental records do not include a York M. King. Cpl. Luke M. King was present at every recorded muster and with the regiment at its surrender in April 1865.

Hd Qrs 2nd Regt Tenn. Cavalry
Maynardsville, July 31st 1862

Capt. Martin & Beagles[105]

Will immediately make preparations and by 10 Oclock A.M. march with their entire company for Wallace X Roads with as much dispatch as practable where they will picket and scout the front of Lt. Col. Carter's position which he has been ordered to leave for the present. Upon Lt. Col. Carter's return they will also return to this point.

Lt. Col. Carter will leave directions as to position of pickets and scouts.

Most Respectfully
J. B. McLin, Col.
Comdg Regt

P. S. The Quarter master will furnish half our transportation to the above companies.

J. B. McLin, Col.[106]

---

[105] Capt. Alvin W. Beegles (Beagles) was elected Captain on May 24, 1865. He deserted December 1, 1863 and took the oath of allegiance at Nashville on December 25. He apparently requested a trial by Confederate authorities on March 31, 1864.

[106] This is the last order issued by Col. McLin. On August 12 he was replaced by George W. McKenzie by order of Gen. Kirby Smith.

Hd Qrs 2nd Regt Tenn. Cav.
Near Cumb. Gap, Aug 2 [?] /62

Special Order }
No. ----- }

      Capt. J. Graham[107] of Co. K 2nd Batt. Tenn. Cav. 3rd Brigade will proceed to --?-- [hold?] an election in his co. at 10 Oclock A.M. this inst [?] to elect a Brevet 2nd Lt. in said company in obedience to an order of the Brigade commander.

                                    By order
                       G. W. McKenzie, Lt. Col.
                             Comdg Batt.
                         R. F. Sloan A. Adjt.

---

[107] John W. Graham was elected Captain on May 24, 1862 and took command on June 1. He was with the regiment at its surrender in April 1865.

Hd Qrs 2nd Batt. Tenn. Cav.
Camp Hunting Creek, August 15th 1862

Special Order
No. I

      Capt. James M. Martin will proceed to take charge of all the commissary stores that Capt. G. H. Bogguss[108] has on hand.

By order of
Lt. Col. G. W. McKenzie
R. F. Sloan, A. Adjt.

---

[108] Pvt. Irby H. Boggess was elected sheriff of Meigs County and Major of the county's militia in September 1862.

                                    Head Qrs 2 Bat. T. Cav.
                                      Roses Forge Sept 5th

Gen'l Order }
No. 1   }

   The following reconstruction in the letters of the Co's of this command takes place from this date.[109] Viz: Capt. Blackwell's Co. becomes Co. "A", Capt. Kincaid's "B", Capt. Martin's "C", Capt. Beegles "D", Capt. Carder's "E", Capt. Mims's "F", Capt. Graham's "G", Capt. Mullendore's "H".

                                       By order of
                                  Lt. Col. G. W. McKenzie
                                       R. F. Sloan, Ajt.

---

[109] These letter designations were retained when the 2nd Battalion became the 5th Regiment on December 16, 1862.

Head Qrs 2nd Bat. Tenn. Cav'y.
Sept 10th 1862

(Copy)

Gen'l Stevenson[110]
    Comdg 1st Div. Dept. E. Tenn.

        Sir

Mr. E. A. Broyles the bearer of this and the Sergt Major of my command desires a detail for the purpose of assisting to make up a company in Washington Co. Mr. Broyles is a very worthy young man and has an offer of a Lieut's place in a co. nearly made up in his county. If you can grant him the detail you will benefit the service & confer a favor on

        Your Obed't Serv't
        G. W. McKenzie, Lt. Col.

If Col. McKenzie's Bat. is full he can detach the applicant for the purpose stated: if not I would suggest to him to use his competent officers & men to fill his ranks.

        C. L. Stevenson
        Brig. Gen'l
        Comdg.

Head Qrs 2nd Bat. Tenn. Cav.
Roses Forge, Sept. 12th 1862

By virtue of the authority endorsed on this application, Sergt Major Broyles[111] herein mentioned is granted leave of absence for Forty days to proceed to Washington Co. for the purposes mentioned in the application.

        G. W. McKenzie, Lt. Col.
        Comdg Bat.

---

[110] Gen. Carter Littlepage Stevenson, a West Point graduate of 1838 and Mexican War veteran, was ordered early in 1862 to the Western theater and took part in Gen. Kirby Smith's invasion of Kentucky in August.

[111] Sgt. Maj. Broyles was unsuccessful if he tried to raise a company for he was detailed as a hospital drugggist at Greeneville on October 10 and later in hospital at Emory, Virginia as a clerk due to ulceration of the legs. He took the oath after war's end at Chattanooga on May 24, 1865.

Hd Qrs 2d Battallion Tenn. Cav
Sept 13, 1862

Charges & specifications against Phillip Wierick,[112] private in Capt. Martin's Co. (C), 2d Battallion Tenn. Cav. 3d Brigade.

Charges

Unsoldierlike conduct.

Specifications

1st Said Phillip Wierick was regularly detailed on the 9th of Sept. 1862 for pickett duty and whilst on post did disgracefully leave & desert his post without permission, contrary to Army Regulations & Articles of War.

W. O. Martin, Capt.
Co. (C) 2d Bat. T. Cav.

Witnesses:
Corpl. T. F. Woods[113]
Private J. B. Nance[114]

---

[112] Pvt. Phillip Warick (or Wyrick) was taken as a substitute for N. L. Cate on July 23, 1862. He was AWOL in late 1862 and left without returning on March 3, 1863, taking the oath at Knoxville on December 29, 1863.

[113] Cpl. Thomas F. Woods took the oath of allegiance on September 25, 1864 as a rebel deserter.

[114] Pvt. James B. Nance was present at the surrender in April 1865.

[*The following entry is lined out*]

                                         Hd Qrs 2nd Bat. Tenn. Cav.
                                              Kingston, Nov. 14th 1862

Capt. J. M. Kincaid[115]

        Sir

                You will procede on Saturday the 15th Inst between the hours of 1 & 3 Oclock P.M. to hold an election in your Co. for a Brevet 2nd Lieut. to fill the vacancy therein existing.

                                          J. G. M. Montgomery, Major
                                          Comdg 2nd Bat. Tenn. Cav.

---

[115] Capt. James M. Kincaid was discharged in August 1863 for disability. In December 1863 he was captured in Roane County and sent to Camp Chase.

Hd Qrs 2nd Batt. Tenn. Cav.
Camp near Kingston Nov 18th 1862

Capt. J. M. Kincaid

    Sir

    You will proceed on Tuesday the 18th inst between the hours of 10 Oclock A.M. & 12 M. to open & hold an election in your company for Brevet 2nd Lieut. to fill the vacancy therein existing.

By order of
G. W. McKenzie, Lt. Col.
Cmmdg Batt.
R. F. Sloan, Adjt.

Hd Qrs 2nd Batt. Tenn. Cavalry
Camp near Kingston, Nov 18th 1862

Special Order }
No.   }

     An election having been held on the 18th Nov., 1862 in accordance with orders Jas. L. Wierick[116] receiving majority is declared elected and is assigned to duty as Brevet 2nd Lieut. Co. (B) 2nd Bat. Tenn. Caval'y.

By order of
Lt. Col. G. W. McKenzie, Comdg.
R. F. Sloan, Adjt.

---

[116] Lt. James L. Wierick was with the regiment at its surrender in April 1865.

Hd Qrs 2nd Batt. Ten. Cav.
Camp near Kingston, Tenn.
Nov. 18th 1862

James A. Day[117] is hereby appointed Steward of the 2nd Batt. Tenn. Cavalry and will rank as such.

Sam'l H. Day, Surgeon
2nd Batt. Tenn. Cavalry

Approved
G. W. McKenzie, Lt. Col.
Commanding 2nd Batt. Ten. Cav.

R. F. Sloan Adjt.

---

[117] No record has been found for James A. Day.

Hd Qrs 5th Regt Tenn. Cav.[118]
Camp near Knoxville, Jan 1st 1863

The commander of Co. (C) will detail Jno. G. McCarty[119] to report to the A. A. Q. M. for duty as forage master.

By order of
G. W. McKenzie, Col.
Comdg Regt
R. F. Sloan, Adjt

---

[118] This is the first order issued from the 5th Regiment.

[119] Regimental records do not include John G. McCarty.

                              Hd Qtrs 5th Regt. Tenn. Cav.
                              Jacksboro, Tenn. Jan 12th 1863

General Orders No. }
                   }

       1st. the commanders of companies have no authority to furlough, detail, or order any N. C. officer or private away from the regt.

2d. All commanders of companies are required to arrest & prefer written charges & specifications against every N. C. officer or private who may be absent without leave, and all those who have absented themselves a second time since the army came out of Kentucky.

3d. Any failure on the part of company commanders to comply with the above orders, the law in all its rigor will be enforced against such officers.

                                        By order
                                   G. W. McKenzie, Col.
                             Comdg, 5th Regt. Tenn. Cav.
                                    R. F. Sloan, Adj.

                                    Hd Qrs 5th Regt. Tenn. Cavalry
                             Maynardsville, Tenn. Feb 11th, 1863

Capt. A. J. Ragan

    Comdg Co. (A) 5th Regt. Tenn. Cav.

                                        You
will proceed to hold an election in your company at 7 Oclock
tomorrow morning to elect a Brevet 2nd Lt. the vacancy having
occured by the promotion of Capt. J. L. Blackwell[120] to Major
of 5th Regt. Tenn. Cav.

                                        G. W. McKenzie, Col.
                                        Comdg 5th Regt. Tenn. Cav.

---

[120] Capt. J. L. Blackwell was promoted to Major December 17, 1862. He resigned January 18, 1864, both hands being injured.

                                    Hd Qrs 5th Regt. Tenn. Cav.
                                    Maynardsville, Feb 12th 1863

In obedience to an order of Col. G. W. McKenzie, Comdg 5th Regt., I proceeded to hold an election for Brevet 2nd Lt. in my company the result of the election is as follows:

M. D. Lansford[121] being the only candidate rec'd thirty-six votes.

                                                    Signed
                                            G. W. Gardner, Clerk

I certify that the above is a true return of an election held in my Co. for Brevet 2nd Lt. at 7 Oclock A.M. Feb 12th 1863.

                                            A. J. Ragan, Capt.
                                                Comdg Company

The said M. D. Lansford is hereby ordered to report to Capt. A. J. Ragan for duty.

                                                    By order
                                            G. W. McKenzie, Col.
                                        Comdg 5th Regt. Tenn. Cav.
                                                    R. F. Sloan
                                                        Adjt.

---

[121] M. D. Lansford was elected Lieutenant February 10, 1863. He was captured August 1, 1863 at Irvine, Kentucky and released from Johnson's Island Prison on June 11, 1865.

                                    Hd Qrs 5th Regt. Tenn. Cav.
                            Camp near Knoxville, Feb 25th 1863

Special Order}
No.   }

        Capt. A. J. Ragan & Lt. S. H. Wilson[122] of Co. A and Lt. W. G. Harner[123] of Co. (G) is hereby appointed a board of survey to value a horse that was killed in action near Harrodsburg, Ky. belonging to private James Taylor[124] of Co. A 5th Regt. Tenn. Cav. and report their action to these Hd Qrs.

                                            By order
                                    G. W. McKenzie, Col.
                                    Cmdg 5th Regt, Tenn. Cav.
                                    R. F. Sloan, Adjt.

In obedience to the above order we the undersigned Board of survey after due consultation and with a first hand knowledge of the said Horse do agree and value the said horse at Two hundred & twenty-five Dollars.

                                            A. J. Ragan, Capt.
                                            S. H. Wilson, Lt.
                                            W. G. Harner, Lt.

---

[122] Lt. Samuel Wilson resigned July 18, 1864, stating that he could not afford to keep himself mounted.

[123] Lt. W. F. Horner's resignation for health reasons was accepted by the president on March 5, 1863.

[124] See Note 66.

                                    Hd Qrs 5th Regt. Tenn. Cav.
                              Camp near Knoxville Feb 28th, 1863

Capt. A. J. Ragan

        You will proceed at once to muster &
inspect Capt. Carder's Co. (E) for the months of Jan'y & Feb.
1863[125].

                                                  By order
                                          J L. Blackwell, Maj.
                                                 Comdg Regt
                                          R. F. Sloan, Adjt.

---

[125] This order for muster and the one following was to pay the soldiers.

                                        Hd Qrs 5th Regt Tenn. Cav.
                            Camp near Knoxville, Feb. 28th 1863

Capt. T. M. Carder

            You will proceed at once to
muster & inspect the following Cos. be'g [being] Cos. A, B,
C, D, F, G, H, I, & K for the months of Jan'y & Feb 1863.

                                                By order
                                        J. L. Blackwell, Maj.
                                                Comdg Regt
                                          R. F. Sloan, Adjt.

[*Loose sheet*]

Headquarters Army Tennessee
Dalton, Ga. March 30, 1864

Gen'l Order }
No. 28   }

I. In pursuance of an act of Congress Entitled "An Act to provide for retiring officers of the Army" published in G O 22 A & I G O 1864 which authorizes the President of the Confederate States upon the recommendation of the General Commanding to "Discharge from service any officer who has no command & cannot be assigned to any appropriate duty, or who is incompetent or inefficient or who may be absent from his command or duty without leave" Commanding officers will report the names of such officers as come within its perview and forward their reports to these Hqrs with the remarks of intermediate commanders -- fairly & fully presenting each case.

II. Each name will be reported on a separate paper and will state the grade, company and Regiment or Battalion of the officer. If absent by what authority & where he may be found, and if absent on duty, what duty & by whose order he may have been assigned.

III. In order that the army may be at once relieved of incompetent & unworthy officers, it is important that these reports should be made promptly.

By command of
General Johnston

Official
(sg) E. S. Burford
      aag

(sg) Kinlock Falcone
      aag

Official
J. W. Frierson, Jr.
      aaag

[*Loose sheet*]

Hd Qrs Humes Brigade
Tunnel Hill Ga. Apr 2, 1864

The reports called for in Gen'l Orders No. 28 Hdqrs Army Tenn. dated Dalton, Ga. March 30, 1864 - will be forwarded without delay to these Hdqrs.

By Order of
Brig Gen'l Humes
J. W. Frierson, Jr.
aaag

Col. G. W. McKenzie
Comdg 5th Tenn. Cav.

ORGANIZATIONAL SUMMARY

Date	Mustered at	From	Company Commander	1st Rgt	2nd Bn	5th Rgt	Company Commander
1861							
Oct 19	Knoxville	Union	Brock	A			
Nov 1	Decatur	Meigs	McKenzie	B	B/C	C	Martin/Blevins
Nov 12	Cleveland	Bradley	Brown	C			
Nov 13	Cleveland	Polk	McClary	D	E	E	Carder
Nov 20	Knoxville	Cocke	Gorman	E	E/F	F	Gorman/Mimms
Aug 24	Knoxville	Hamilton, Ala, Ga	White	F	F/A	A	Reagan
Oct 21	Knoxville	Washington, Greene	McLin	G	H	H	Mullendore
1862							
Jan 27	Knoxville	Roane, Meigs, McMinn	Kincaid	H	H/B	B	Kincaid/Blythe
Feb 14	Cleveland	Bradley	Montgomery	I	I/D	D	Beagles
Mar 31	Knoxville	An independent Co.	Jones	K	K/G	G	Graham
Jul 19	Shiloh	Meigs, Hamilton	Lillard		I	I	Lillard
Jul 4	Maryville	North Carolina Co.	Ghormley		F/K	K	Ghormley

Brock's Company mustered out April 12, 1862
Brown's Company transferred on May 16, 1862 to 63rd Tenn Inf Regt as Company H
Lillard's Company joined 2nd/13th Battalion on Oct 9, 1862
Ghormley's Company joined 2nd/13th Battalion on Dec 16, 1862

1st (Rogers) Tennessee Cavalry Regiment

Also known as: 1st (Rogers') East Tennessee Cavalry Regiment
2nd (McLin's) Tennessee Cavalry Regiment
2nd Tennessee Cavalry Battalion
13th Tennessee Cavalry Battalion

Colonels: John F. Rogers, John B. McLin
Lt. Cols: John F. White, George W. McKenzie
Majors: John B. McLin, John G. M. Montgomery

Jan 7, 1862 Organized
May 24   Re-organized with 8 companies
Aug 12   Reduced to Battalion. Known as 2nd, also as 13th Battalion
Dec 16   Raised to Regiment by adding 2 companies. Designated 5th McKenzie's

5th (McKenzie's) Tennessee Cavalry Regiment

Colonels: George W. McKenzie (formerly Lt. Col., 13th Battalion)
Lt. Cols: John G. M. Montgomery (formerly Major, 13th Battalion)
Majors: J. L. Blackwell (formerly Captain, Co. A, 13th Battalion)

SUMMARY OF ORDERS

Date	Name	Location	Order	Officer	Adjutant
1862					
Feb 5		Knoxville	SO 19	Leadbetter	
Feb 27	1st Regt	Jacksborough	GO 1	White	Davenport
Feb 28	1st Regt	Jacksboro	SO 4	Rodgers	
Mar 1		Jacksboro		Rodgers	
Mar 2	1st Regt	Jacksboro		Rodgers	
Mar 3	1st Regt		GO 2	Rogers	Davenport
Mar 3	1st Regt	Camp Skooler	SO	White	
Mar 3	1st Regt	Jacksboro	SO 5	Rogers	Davenport
Mar 3	1st Regt	Jacksboro	SO 6	Rogers	Davenport
Mar 3	1st Regt		SO 7	Rogers	
Mar 3	1st Regt	Jacksboro	SO 8	Rogers	
Mar 3	1st Regt		SO 9	Rogers	
Mar 3	1st Regt		SO 10	Rogers	
Mar 3	1st Regt		SO 11	Rogers	
Mar 3	1st Regt		SO 12	Rogers	
	1st Regt		SO 13	Rogers	
Mar 3	1st Regt		SO 14	Rogers	
Mar 3	1st Regt		SO 15	Rogers	
Mar 3	1st Regt		SO 16	Rogers	
Mar 3	1st Regt		SO 17	Rogers	
Mar 4	1st Regt	Jacksboro	SO 18	Wheeler	
Mar 4	1st Regt	Jacksboro	SO 19	Rogers	Davenport
Mar 4	1st Regt	Jacksboro	SO 20	Rogers	
Mar 5	1st Regt		SO 21	Rogers	Davenport
Mar 5	1st Regt		SO 22	Rogers	Davenport
Mar 3	1st Regt		SO 23	Rogers	Davenport
Mar 3			SO 24	Rogers	Davenport
Mar 3	1st Regt	Jacksboro	SO 25	Rogers	
Mar 6	1st Regt	Jacksboro	GO 3	White	Davenport
Mar 6	1st Regt	Jacksborough	GO 4	White	Davenport
Mar 6	1st Regt	Jacksboro	SO 26	White	Davenport
Mar 6	1st Regt	Jacksboro	SO 27	White	Davenport
Mar 7	1st Regt		SO 28	White	Davenport
Mar 8	1st Regt	Jacksboro	SO 29	White	
Mar 8	1st Regt	Jacksboro	SO 30	White	Davenport
Mar 9	1st Regt	Jacksboro	SO 31	White	Davenport
Mar 9	1st Regt		SO 32	White	
Mar 9	1st Regt		SO 33	White	
Mar 9	1st Regt	Jacksborough	SO 34	White	
Mar 9	1st Regt	Jacksboro	GO 5	White	
Mar 11	1st Regt	Jacksboro	SO 35	White	Davenport
Mar 11	1st Regt			White	
Mar 11	1st Regt	Jacksboro	SO 36	White	
Mar 11	1st Regt	Jacksboro	SO 37	White	Davenport
Mar 11	1st Regt			White	
Mar 12	1st Regt		GO 6	White	

Date	Unit	Location	Order	Signed	Other
Mar 13	1st Regt	Jacksboro	SO 38	White	Davenport
Mar 13			SO 39	White	
Mar	1st Regt	Jacksboro	SO 40	Montgomery	
May 31		Kingston	GO	McLin	
Jun 8		Kingston	SO	McLin	
Jun 9		Kingston	GO	--?--	
Jun 18	1st Regt	Camp Allston			Broyles
Jun 22	1st Regt	Camp Allston		McKenzie	Broyles
Jul 1	1st Regt	Camp Allston		McLin	Sloan
Jul 4	1st Regt	Maynardsville	SO	McLin	
Jul 12	2nd Regt	Maynardsville	SO	McLin	
Jul 18	2nd Regt	Maynardsville		McLin	
Jul 18	2nd Regt	Maynardsville	SO	McLin	
Jul 20	2nd Regt	Maynardsville	SO	McLin	
Jul 20	2nd Regt	Maynardsville		McLin	Sloan
Jul 20	2nd Regt	Maynardsville	SO	McLin	
Jul 22	2nd Regt	Maynardsville	SO	McLin	
Jul 31	2nd Regt	Maynardsville		McLin	
Aug 2	2nd Regt	Cumberland Gap	SO	McKenzie	Sloan
Aug 15	2nd Batt	Hunting Creek	SO I	McKenzie	Sloan
Sep 5	2nd Batt	Roses Forge	GO 1	McKenzie	Sloan
Sep 10	2nd Batt	Roses Forge		McKenzie	
Sep 13	2nd Batt			Martin	
Nov 14	2nd Batt	Kingston		Montgomery	
Nov 18	2nd Batt	Kingston		McKenzie	Sloan
Nov 18	2nd Batt	Kingston	SO	McKenzie	Sloan
Nov 18	2nd Batt	Kingston		McKenzie	Sloan

1863

Date	Unit	Location	Order	Signed	Other
Jan 1	5th Regt	Knoxville		McKenzie	Sloan
Jan 12	5th Regt	Jacksboro	GO	McKenzie	Sloan
Feb 11	5th Regt	Maynardsville		McKenzie	
Feb 12	5th Regt	Maynardsville		McKenzie	Sloan
Feb 25	5th Regt	Knoxville	SO	McKenzie	Sloan
Feb 28	5th Regt	Knoxville		Blackwell	Sloan
Feb 28	5th Regt	Knoxville		Blackwell	Sloan

1864

Date	Unit	Location	Order	Signed
Mar 30	Army/Tenn	Dalton	GO 28	Johnston
Apr 2	Humes Brg	Tunnel Hill		Humes

INDEX TO ORDERS AND NOTES

1st East Tennessee Cavalry Regiment   53n
1st Tennessee Cavalry Battalion   4n
1st (Rogers') Tennessee Cavalry Regiment   1n, 2, 3, 5, 6, 7,
    8, 9, 10, 11, 12, 13, 14, 15, 16, 17, 18, 19, 20, 21, 22,
    23, 24, 25, 26, 28, 29, 30, 31, 32, 33, 34, 35, 36, 37,
    38, 39, 40, 44, 47, 48, 49, 50,   51, 52, 53, 54, 55, 56,
    59, 60, 61, 62
2nd (McLin's) Tennessee Cavalry Battalion   4n, 72, 73, 74,
    74n, 75, 76, 77, 78, 79, 80
2nd (McLin's) Tennessee Cavalry Regiment   4n, 64, 64n, 65,
    65n, 66, 67, 68, 69, 70, 71, 72
3rd (Lillard's) Tennessee Infantry Regiment   5n, 36n
3rd Brigade   76
3rd Confederate Cavalry   42n
4th (Branner's) Tennessee Cavalry Battalion   4n, 5
5th (McClellan's) Tennessee Cavalry Battalion   4n
5th (McKenzie's) Tennessee Cavalry Regiment   2n, 3n, 4n, 8n,
    22n, 24n, 26n, 27n, 32n, 74n, 81, 81n, 82, 83, 84, 85,
    86, 87, 89
9th (Malone's) 9th Alabama Cavalry   43n
14th (Carter's) Tennessee Cavalry Battalion   65n
49th Indiana Volunteers   54n
63rd Tennessee Infantry Regiment   12n, 36n, 53n

Alexander, Sgt. S. H.   3, 3n, 39
Allen, W. G.   28n
Allston, Col. Benjamin   59n, 66n
Army of Tennessee   88, 89
Ashby, Col. Henry M.   65, 65n

Baker, Lt. John   40, 50n, 54, 54n
Bates, John M.   12, 12n, 35, 35n
Beagles; See Beegles
Bean's Station   65n
Beegle's Company   74
Beegles, Capt. Alvin W.   71, 71n
Beeler, Lt.   2, 2n
Beeler, Pvt. John   2n
Beeler, Sgt. L. B.   2n
Belton, AAG J. B.   60n
Benton, Pvt. Little Page Sims   44, 44n
Big Creek Gap   28, 36n, 54n
Blackwell's Company   74
Blackwell, Capt./Maj. J. L.   2, 2n, 3, 65, 83, 83n, 86, 87
Blancet, Pvt. G. H.   40, 40n, 42, 44, 45
Blevins, James D.   69, 69n

Boggess, Pvt. Irby H.   73, 73n
Boggues; See Boggess
Boggus; See Boggess
Bradley County   8n, 32n
Bridgeman, Maj. John M.   4, 4n, 5
Brittain, Benjamin F.   53, 53n
Britten; See Brittain
Brock's Company   22n, 53n
Brock, Capt. A. J.   2, 2n, 22n, 23, 53
Brown's Company   12n, 53n, 54n
Brown, Capt. William L.   25n, 31, 34, 34n, 53
Broyles, Edwin A.   15, 15n, 59, 60, 75
Bruce, Mr.   38
Burford, E. S.   88

Camp Allston   59, 60, 61
Camp Chase   3n, 77n
Camp Hunting Creek   73
Camp Maynardsville   64
Camp Schooler   1n, 7, 7n
Camp Skooler; See Camp Schooler
Campbell County   1n
Cannon, Cpl./Sgt. Robert   3, 3n, 39, 42
Carder's Company   74, 86
Carder, Capt. Thaddeus M.   87
Carroll, Gen. William Henry   1n
Carter, Col. James P. T. (USA)   54n
Carter, Lt. Col. James E.   65, 65n, 71
Cate, N. L.   76n
Chattanooga   39n, 75n
Chickamauga, Tennessee   3n
Chitwood Gap   7
Clay, AAG H. L.   56n, 61n, 65n, 66
Clemmer, G. W.   5n
Cleveland, Tennessee   20, 28n
Clinch River   7, 50, 65
Clinton Road   45
Clinton, Tennessee   2
Cocke County   2n
Company A   2n, 3n, 22, 22n, 24n, 74, 83, 85, 87
Company B   2n, 10, 18, 22, 22n, 62, 69, 70, 74, 79, 87
Company C   2n, 11, 12, 22n, 25, 25n, 61n, 74, 76, 81, 87
Company D   8n, 9, 19, 27, 27n, 32n, 33, 74, 87
Company E   26, 26n, 27n, 32, 40, 54, 55, 65, 74, 86
Company F   2n, 3, 17, 21, 24, 24n, 26n, 32, 37, 40, 42, 43, 44, 45, 50, 65, 74, 87
Company G   15, 22, 22n, 65, 74, 85, 87
Company H   2n, 22n, 53n, 74, 87
Company I   8n, 32, 32n, 40, 47, 54, 55, 87
Company K   64, 65, 72, 87
Confederate States   3, 39
Cooksten; See Croxton
Cooper, Gen. Samuel   1n, 54n
Coxey; See Coxsey
Coxsey, Lt. John B.   31n

Crews, Tolliver 43, 43n, 45, 46
Crittenden, Gen. George Bibb 1n
Crossville, Tennessee 56n
Croxton, Cpl. E. H. 3, 3n, 39
Cruce; See Crews
Cumberland Gap 2, 61n, 72

Dalton, Georgia 88, 89
Davenport, Monteville D. 2, 6, 8, 9, 14, 14n, 22, 24, 25, 26,
    27, 29, 30, 31, 32, 33, 35, 36, 41, 42, 43, 47, 51, 53
Davenport, Pvt. J. G. 43, 43n
Day, James A. 80, 80n
Day, Samuel H. 80
Department of East Tennessee 75
Dobbins, Pvt. James 40, 40n, 42, 43, 44
Dobbins, Pvt. William 40, 40n, 44, 45
East Tennessee 1n, 5n, 40n, 50
East Tennessee Cavalry Battalion 4n
Edwards, Joseph 16n
Emory, Virginia 75n

Falcone[r], Kinlock 88
Fincastle 65
Fishing Creek 2n
Ford, Dr. George W. 20, 20n
Frierson, J. W. 88, 89

Gardner, G. W. 84
Georgia Cavalry 58
Gorman's Company 7, 7n
Gorman, Capt. Thomas S. 2, 2n, 26n
Graham's Company 74
Graham, Capt. John W. 72, 72n
Graham, Mr. 28, 28n
Grahamville, S. C. 3n
Greeneville, Tennessee 75n

Hale, Pvt. William F. 39, 39n, 43
Harner; See Horner
Harris, Gov. Isham 5n
Harrodsburg, Kentucky 85
Holt, Pvt. Robert S. 11, 11n
Horner, Lt. W. F. 85, 85n
Hoyl, Lt. Thomas M. 36, 36n, 54n
Huges; See Hughes
Hughes, Cpl. Joshua 3, 3n, 39
Humes' Brigade 89
Humes, Gen. W. Y. C. 40n, 89
Huntsville Road 47, 55

Irvine, Kentucky 84n

Jacksboro 2, 3, 4, 5, 7, 7n, 8, 9, 11, 21, 22, 23, 28, 29,
    30, 31, 32, 34, 35, 36, 39, 40, 47, 50, 51, 53, 54, 55,
    82

Jacksborough; See Jacksboro
Jamestown Road 5
Jarnigan, John 4, 4n
Jarnigin; See Jarnigan
Jenkins, Cpl. 3
Johnson's Island Prison 84n
Johnston, Gen. Joseph E. 88

Kentucky, State of 2n, 50, 75n, 82
Kincaid's Company 74
Kincaid, Capt. James M. 77, 77n, 78
Kincer; See Kinser
King, Cpl. Luke M. 70n
King, York M. 70, 70n
Kingston 53n, 56, 56n, 57, 57n, 58, 59, 61, 61n, 77, 78, 79, 80
Kinser, A. J. 53n
Kinson, Lt. Al 53
Knoxville 1, 1n, 2, 2n, 5, 7, 7n, 9, 21, 50, 54n, 56n, 60n, 61n, 65, 65n, 66, 66n, 76n, 81, 85, 86, 87

Lansford, M. D. 84, 84n
Leadbetter, Col./Gen. Daniel 1, 1n, 7n, 53n, 54n, 56n
Lindmen; See Lindner
Lindner, Pvt. Frederick E. 13, 13n
Lloyd's Crossroads 60n
Louden 5
Lowery, Cpl./Sgt. W. T. 3, 3n, 39
Lowry; See Lowery

Martin's Company 74, 76
Martin, Capt. W. O. 67, 67n, 71, 76
Martin, James M. 10, 10n, 11, 73
Maynardsville 61n, 62, 65, 66, 67, 68, 69, 70, 71, 83, 84
Maynardsville Road 2
McCarty, John G. 81, 81n
McClary's Company 31n, 54n
McClary, Pvt. Charles M. 19, 19n
McClary, Robert W. 27n
McKenzie's Company 7n
McKenzie, Capt./Col. George W. 2, 2n, 7, 22n, 60, 65, 71n, 72, 73, 74, 75, 78, 79, 80, 81, 82, 83, 84, 85, 89
McLin, Maj./Col. John B. 22, 22n, 56, 57, 57n, 60n, 61, 61n, 63, 64, 64n, 65, 65n, 66, 67, 68, 69, 70, 71, 71n
McMahan, Lt. McKinney 55, 55n
McMahan, R. A. 16, 16n, 18
Meigs County 2n, 73n
Mexican War 2n, 75n
Mims' Company 74
Mims, Capt. A. L. 65, 65n, 66, 66n
Montgomery, Capt./Maj. John George Morgan 8, 8n, 32n, 40, 44, 46, 55, 56n, 77
Montgomery, Tennessee 5, 7n, 57n
Moreland, Dr. L. C. 17, 17n
Morgan County 1n, 7n

Mullendore's Company 74
Munster's Ford 65
Mynatt's Cross Roads 65n

Nance, Pvt. James B. 76, 76n
Nashville 71n

O'Neal, John L. 9, 9n, 56
O'Neal, John S.; See O'Neal, John L.
O'Neil, James S.; See O'Neal, John L.
Ohio, State of 54n

Philips, Elias; See Phillips, Ellis
Phillips, Ellis 42, 42n
Powell's Valley 65

Ragan; See Reagan, A. J.
Ragon, Z. L.; See Reagan, Z. H.
Reagan, Pvt. Z. H. 69, 69n
Reagan, Sgt./Capt. A. J. 3, 3n, 39, 83, 84, 85, 86
Reagon; See Reagan, A. J.
Richmond, Virginia 1n, 54n
Roane County 77n
Roberts, Lt. P. G. 3, 3n, 39
Robertsville 5
Rodgers, Col. John F.; See Rogers
Rogers, Col. John F. 3, 4, 5, 6, 8, 9, 10, 11, 12, 13, 14, 15, 16, 17, 18, 19, 20, 21, 22, 23, 24, 25, 26, 27, 28, 28n
Rogers, Mr. 28, 28n
Rose's Forge 74, 75

Scott County 1n, 53n
Sharps 45
Shepherd, Philo 51, 51n
Sloan, Lt. 47
Sloan, Lt. Felix P. 40, 47n, 54
Sloan, Lt. Robert F. 40, 44, 46, 47n, 54, 61, 61n, 68, 72, 73, 74, 78, 79, 80, 81, 82, 84, 85, 86, 87
Sloan, William E. 5n, 61n
Smith, Gen. E. Kirby 54n, 60n, 71n, 75n
Stevenson, Gen. Carter Littlepage 60n, 65n, 75, 75n

Taswell [Tazewell] 61n
Taylor, Pvt./Cpl. James 3, 3n, 39, 39n, 85
Taylor, Pvt. Jesse 3n
Tunnel Hill, Georgia 2n, 89

Union County 2n

Vaughn, Col. John C. 5, 5n
Vicksburg, Mississippi 36n
Virginia, State of 5n

Wallace's Cross Roads 40n, 61n, 65, 65n, 71

Warick, Pvt. Philip 76, 76n
Washington County 75
West Point Academy 75n
Wheeler, Lt. James C. 3, 3n, 21, 37, 40, 48, 49
Wheler; See Wheeler
White's Company 3n
White, Capt./Lt. Col. John F. 2, 2n, 7, 7n, 21, 24, 24n, 25,
    26, 27, 29, 30, 31, 32, 33, 34, 35, 36, 36n, 37, 38, 39,
    40, 44, 46, 47, 48, 49, 50, 51, 52, 53, 54, 54n
White, Pvt. W. C. 3n
White, Sgt./Lt. George C. 3, 21, 21n
Wierick, James L. 79
Wierick, Lt. James L. 79n
Wierick, Phillip; See Warick
Willets; See Willett
Willett, George W. 2, 2n
Williams, Pvt. Robert L. 70, 70n
Williamsburg, Ky. 7
Williamson, John W. C. 64n
Wilson, Lt. Samuel H. 85, 85n
Woods, Cpl. Thomas F. 76, 76n
Wyrick; See Warick

PART 2 — COPIES OF ORIGINAL ORDERS

Special Order No 4
                    Head Quarters First Regt Tenn
            Jackstown Tenn 28 Feb 1862

In accordance with Military Law and the Army Regulations of the Confederate States The Offices vacated by promotion will be filled by promotion from the grades below. In Company F of the Regiment 1st Lieut L Blackwell becomes the Capt 2nd Lieut Wheeler 1st Lieut Lieut Roberts Second Lieut 1st Sargt G. L. White Jund 2nd Lieut Second Sargent Reagan 1st Sargent 3 Sargt Alexander 2nd Sargt 4th Sargt Lowry 3 Sargt 1st Corporal Cannon 4th Sargent 2nd Corporal Jenkins 1st Corporal 3 Corporal Hugao 2nd Corporal 4th Corporal Taylor 3 Corporal. And E H Cocks 4th Corporal And their Commission to date from the 28th of Jan 1862.

By Order of Jno F Rodgers
            Col Comd Regt
2 O rd tomch

Special Order Head Quarters 1st Reg't Kav.
Camp Rhodes 3rd Mar 1863

Capt. McKenzie will take up his line of
march toward Jacksboro Ten at 12 Oclock Feb'y 4"
1863. He will take with him Capt Gorman's com'y
after establishing the command judiciously
at or near Jacksboro he will proceed to
reconnoiter the country in the direction of
Williamsburg Ky and Chitwood Gap, if
possible will immediately communicate
with ___ giving any information he may
get of the movements of the enemy. If
any superior force threaten his command he
will fall back on the South side of Clinch
River, and destroy all the Boats. Canoes
and Bridges on the River above Clinton.
He will use great diligence to prevent a
Surprise, keeping a heavy Picket-Guard
night and day.
By Order of
J. F. White Col
Comm'd'g

Head Quarters 1st Reg. Tenn.
Jacksborough Jan. 27, Feb. 1.

Gen Orders No. 1.

There will be a detail of five men from each Company as Pickett guards who will at eight oclock move out on the various roads at least 3 miles from town and remain on duty untill 11 oclock A.M. They will then be relieved by a picket of 3 from each company who will remain on duty scouting out for four miles and remain on duty untill relieved at 8 oclock P.M.

Lieut Beeler will act as officer of the guard to night will visit the various post at least twice through the night. Capt. M. Kinzie will furnish the officer of the Day tomorrow who will take charge of the new guard and relieve Lieut Beeler precisely at 6 oclock A.M. Capt Brooks men will guard on the Maynardsville Road, Capt Willets the Mountain Road, Capt Gorman the Road to Cumberland Gap, Capt Blackwell Road to Clinton Capt McKinzie Road to Knoxville. The regular stable guard in each company in addition to the above.

By order of J.F. White Lieut Col
Commanding Battallion
Nathaniel Davenport Adjt.

Head Quaters 1st Reg Ten Cav
Jacksboro Tenn

Maj Jno. M. Bridgeman
Commanding 4 Ten Battalion
Sir

Your Command   You will halt
your Command and fall Back to
Robertsville or Montgomery Keeping out
a Pickett force on the Jamestown
road leading from Knoxville to
Montgomery Report by Courier to
this Commander at Knoxville
of any movements of th enemy you
will also Communicate with Col
Vaughn at Jacksboro any information
you get of the movements of the
enemy you will also Report by
Courier to this Head Quaters
Very Respy
Jno. F. Rodgers
Col

Head Quaters
Jacksboro Mar 1st/62

Jno Gaines
Sir
You will deliver to
Maj Bridgeman Command such
Commissary Stores as he takes with his
Command Taking Receipts for Same
Respy yours
Jno. F. Rodgers
Col Comd

Special Order No 5

Head Quarters 1st Regt Ten Cavalry
Jacksboro March 3 1862

Capt J G M Montgomery
Sir

You will parade your company at 9 O'clock A.M. and proceed to the election of commissioned and non-commissioned Officers of your company reporting the results to these Head quarters, & if no choice is effected at the first balloting you will still continue until a choice is made.

By order of
J T Rogers Col
M Davenport Adjutant

Special Order No 6

Head Quarters 1 Regt Ten Cav
Jacksborough Ten March 3 1862

James S McM Conway, S
Will proceed to Knoxville and procure supplies from the commanding quarter master and Commissary Stores for Regiment & hereby authorized to sign any and all receipts and make requisitions therefor and to do any act or all compel things and acts to enable him to procure Coffee candles sugar Salt Flour horse shoes nails or iron powder shott caps guns saddles bridles Pistols Blankets, & &c

By order of
J T Rogers Col
M Davenport Adjutant

General Order Head Quarters 1 Reg[t]
No. 2   3 March 1862

The commanders of companys of this Regiment will
parrade their entire forces at 11 O'Clock A.M.
and make a close inspection of the arms
belonging thereto and report to these Head
Quarters. By order of   Jno. F. Rogers Col.
                               M Davenport Ajt

Head Quarters
Knoxville Feby 9th 1862

Special Order
(No 19)

I. All officers are prohibited from granting furloughs.
Furloughs already given are hereby revoked, and
all absentees are required to report to their proper
officers for duty without delay —

II. Requisitions for Subsistance cannot be approved
unless approved accompanied by a morning report
of the Commands.

III. Business will be transacted at Head quarters from
9 A.M. to 4 P.M. only —   D Leadbetter
                            Col Commd[g]

Head Quarters 1st Reg[t] Tenn Cavalry
                            March 3 1862
Special Order No 7

Sgt. M. Martin (of company B)
                            Sir you are hereby
detailed to act as commissary for the Reg[t] until
further orders from these Head quarters
                    By order of
                            Jno F Rogers Col

Head Quarters 1st Regt Tenn Cavalry
Special order No 8   Jacksboro March 3rd 1862

Robert S Holt of company B
is hereby detailed to assist Jas. H. Martin acting commissary for the Regiment untill farther orders from these Head quarters.
By order of
Jno F. Rogers
Commanding Post

Head Quarters
1st Regt Tenn Cavalry Mar 3/62
Special order No 10

Fredrick R Lindner (Of company D)
Is hereby detailed to act as assistant Quarter Master for the Regt. untill farther orders from these Head quarters.
By order of Jno F Rogers Col

Special Order No 9   Head Quarters
1st Regt Tenn Cavalry Mar 3

M. Bates (Of Company C)
Is hereby detailed to act as Quarter Master for this Regt. untill farther orders from these Head quarters.
By order of
Jno F. Rogers Col.

Special order No 11   Head Quarters 1st Regt Tenn Cav
March 3rd 1862

N. Davenport (Of Co E)
Is hereby detailed to act as Adjutant for this Regt. untill farther orders from these Head quarters.
By order of Jno F Rogers Col

Special Order No 13
    Head Quarters 1st Regt Tenn Cavalry
      March 3rd 1862

Edwin F. Broyles (of Company G.) is hereby detailed to act as Sergt Major for this Regt until farther orders from these Head-quarters.
    By order of
     Jno. F. Rogers, Col.

Special Order No 13
    Head Quarters 1st Regt Tenn Cavly

R. A. McMahan
  Acting Forrage Master

You will upon the arrival of trains of Forrage waggons report them to the public Store house for unloading, and deliver it out only upon the proper requisition.
    Approved by order of
     Jno F. Rogers, Col
     Comdg Post.

Special Order No 14
    Head Quarters 1st Regt Tenn Cavalry
      March 3 1862

Dr. L. C. Moreland (of Company F) is hereby detailed to act as Asst. Surgeon until farther orders from these Head quarters.
    By order of
     Jno. F. Rogers, Col.

Special order No 15.   Head Quarters
                      1st Regt Tenn Cavalry Mar 3/

R. R. McMahan of company E,
                        Is hereby
detailed to act as Forage Master for this Regt
until farther orders from these Head quarters
                        By order of
                        Jno F Rogers Col
                        Commdg Post

Special order No 16.
                      Head Quarters 1st Regt Tenn Cavalry
                              March 3, 1862

Chas. McClary, of Company D,
                        Is hereby detailed
to act as Waggon master for this Regt Untill farther
orders from these Head quarters—
                        By order of
                        Jno. F. Rogers Col.

Special Order No 17.
                      Head Quarters 1 Reg Tenn Cav
                              3. March 1862

Dr Leon W. Floyd
        Cleveland
                You are hereby appointed
Surgeon of this Regiment untill farther orders
from these Head Quarters and will report yourself to the Head Quarters of this Reg immediately
                        By Order of
                        J. F. Rogers Col
                        Commanding Post

107

Special order No 18   Head Quarters 1 Reg Ten Cavalry
                       Jacksboro Mar 4 1862

Lt Geo. C White, Co D,
                    Sir, you are hereby
required to report yourself for duty to these Head
quarters immediately, you will show this order to
the commanding officer at Knoxville.
                              By order of
Approved by J F Rogers Col   Lt F. E. Wheeler 1st Lt
By J F White Lt Col   Comm'g Company

Special order No 19   Head Quarters 1 Reg Ten Cav'y
                       Jacksboro Mar 4 1862

       The commanders of companies A B & G will
parade their men at Head quarters precisely at
11 oclock to day, and report to Maj McLin for final
marching orders, taking their entire camp equippage
with them.   By order of
                              J F Rogers Col
Special Order No 20   M B Davenport Adjt

                Head Quarters 1st Regt Ten Cavalry
                       Jacksboro Mar 4 1862

Capt A J Brock will make a requisition for
20,000 G D Caps, 100 lb Rifle powder, Buck shot and
Lead, and for to these Head Quarters immediatly.
                       By order of
                              Jno F Rogers
                                Com'g

Special Order No 21 Head Quarters 1st Rgt Ten Cav
March 5" 1862

The commander of Company "F" will furnish Twenty five effective men at 8½ O'clock to be placed under comm'd of Lt Col White.

By order of
Jno. F. Rogers Col
M Davenport Ajt

Special order No 22 Head Quarters 1st Reg't T Cav
March 5" 1862

The commandr of com'y "C" will furnish Forty men at 8½ O'clock to day to be placed under comm'd of Lt Col White,

By order of
Jno F Rogers Col
M Davenport Ajt

Special order No 23 Head Quarters 1st Reg T Cav
March 3 1862

The commander of com'y "E" will furnish twenty men at 8½ O'clock AM to be placed under com'd of Lt Col White.

By order of
Jno F Rogers Col
M Davenport Ajt

Special order No 24 March 3rd 1862

The comm'd of com'y "D" will furnish Thirty men to be placed under com'd of Lt Col White to day at 8½ O'clock;

By order of
Jno F Rogers Col
M Davenport Ajt

Head Quarters 1st Reg't Cavalry
Special Order No. 20 25   Jacksboro March 5

The pickets at Big Creek Gap will pass Mr.
Graham & Rogers through their lines unmolested
By Order of
Jno. F. Royall

Gen'l Order No 3
Head Quarters 1st Reg't Tenn. Cav'y
Jacksboro March 5, 1862

The comm'g officers of the respective companies
belonging to this Reg't are hereby required to make
out a detail for Pickets the night before, and
see that they report themselves at this Head Quarters
precisely at 6 o'clock A.M.
By Order of
J. F. White Lt. Col. comd'g
H. Davenport Adj't

General Order   Head Quarters 1 Reg Ten Cav
No 4   6th March 180. Jacksboro 1862

Commanders of companies are hereby
commanded use their best endeavors to have the sabres
sharpened at the earliest opportunity detailing a
suitable non commissioned officer to superintend
in each company. By Order of
Lieut Col J. F. White
H Davenport, Adj't

Head Quarters 1st Rgt T. Cavalry
Special Order No 26   Jacksboro Mar 5 1862

Capt Brown & Lieut Covey will put their companys in marching orders precisely at 8 oclk tomorrow morning. Each will apply to Qr Master for transportation for company equipage, and for 25 Cartridges per company, and 1/2 lb Blasting Powder. The officers will apply at Head quarters at 2 Oclock today for instructions.

By order of
J. F. White Lieut Col
M Davenport Adjt

Special Order No 27   Head Quarters 1st Rgt T. Cav
Jacksboro Mar 6 1862

The comm'ds of company's "E", "F", & "J" will furnish Thirty five men in the morning to be distributed as follows. Co E Eight, Co F Seventeen and Co J Ten, all of which will be required to be ready to march precisely at 8½ Oclock A.M.

By order of
J. F. White Lt Col
M Davenport Adjt

Special Order No 28   Head Quarters 1st Rgt T Cav
Mar 7 1862

The comm'ds of companys C & D will put their companys in marching orders precisely at 8 Oclock A.M. instead of 8½ Oclock A.M. as previously ord.

By order of
J. F. White Lt Col Com
M Davenport Adjt

Samuel Bennett

Head Quarters 1st Reg't Tn Cav
Spl order no 29   Jacksboro   Mar 8th 1862

Capt W L Brown has leave of absence from camps and is relieved of camp duties until the 18th inst. at which time he will report himself at Regimental Head quarters for duty.   By order of J F White
                                                Lt Col Comm'g

Head Quters 1st Reg't T Cav
Special order no 30,   Jacksboro Mar 8th 1862

Capt Ino Cates Act'g Regimental Qr Master
                        Sir, You are hereby authorized to hire a sufficient no of waggons to haul hay and corn for the reg't in addition to Gov't Teams now under your control, and may bind the Government to pay the following prices, That is to Say, For a
(Pair) Two horse team and waggon   300
    Three   "   "   "   3.50
    Four   "   "   "   4.00

With 50¢ per day to the driver of the team, if you cannot hire teams at these prices you are authorized to appraise & to press them wherever you can find them with discretion in the exercise of the duty. You will pay the owners of forsaid teams in accordance with the above rates of hire.   By order of J F White Lt Col
                                                M Davenport Adjt

Spl order no 31   Head Quarters 1st Reg't T Cav
                        Jacksboro Mar 9 1862

Thom M Hoyl is detailed as Bearer of despatches to Knoxville.   By order of J F White Lt Col
                                                Com'g M Davenport Adjt

112

Special Order 32   Head Quarters 1 Regiment Ten cav
                    9 March 1862

Lieut J. C. Wheeler
        Commanding Company (F)
                    Sir you will take
steps to put your company under marching
orders.
                    By order of
                    J. F. White, Lt. Col.

Special Order No. 33   Head Quarters 1 Reg Ten Cav
                        9 March 1862

Mr Bruce
        Sir information having been received
at these Head Quarters that you are selling
Whiskey to soldiers belonging to this command
I hereby notify you that if you sell
or give any more Liquors to the men I
will cause you to be brought to this
place and inflict upon you the severest
punishment of the law for such offences
                    J. F. White
                    Lt Col Commanding

Special Order No 34   Head Quarters 1th Reg Tenn Cav
                       Jacksborough 9 March 1862

        In accordance with the Regulations
of the Army of the Confederate States the vacancy
occasioned in commissioned officers by the Resignation
of Lieut D. J. Roberts will be filled by regular
promotion from the officers below first Sergeant J.
Heager will become 2 Lieut Sergt Jno. D. Sup
Alexander 1st Sergt 3 Sergt L---- 2nd
Sergt 4 Sergt C--- 5 Sergt 1 Corp
4 Sergt 2 Corp Hugh 1 Corp 3 Sergt
1 Davis 4 Corporal

4th Corporal Crotser 5 & Corporal and Private Wm H. Hole is Promoted and appointed 4th Corporal by order of J. F. White Lt Col
Command'g Reg't

Genl Order No. 5
Proceedings of a general court martial convened at Jacksboro, by virtue of the following order.
Head Quarters 1 Reg't In Camp
Jacksboro Mar 9th 1862

A general court martial will assemble at the Court House at 12 O'clock P. M. on the 9th Inst. for the trial of James T. Wm. Dotins and such others as may be brought before it.

Detail for the Court.
Capt. Montgomery Reg't Cavalry Co "I" Pres't of the court. Lieut J. C. Wheeler Co "F"
                                    J. M. Bates   "E"
                    Lieut J. P. Sloan   "I"

Lieut R. F. Sloan of comp'y "I" is appointed Judge advocate of the court.
By comm'd of J. F. White
Lieut Col

Charges against James Dotins — First for becoming intoxicated while on Picket duty 2nd for leaving his Post while on said duty without permission from any Officer sworn to relieve him and strictly leaving the Post unguarded. James Dotins pleads not guilty. Testimony of J. M. Blount private in Co. "F" Question by Judge advocate. Did you see James Dotins on the 8th March intoxicated? Answer. Yes. Was he on Picket duty? Ans. Yes —

114

Did you see him at the Still house? ans yes
Did he stat to you where he got his liquor?
ans at the Still house. Where was he on Picket?
ans at the forks of the road. How far is the Still-house
from the Post? ans. about 1 mile. Was he relieved
by any one before he left? Ans. No. Did he leave the
Post till you relieved? ans. yes.

Cross questioned by Apt Devenport. Was you Sergt
that day? ans. yes. Were you not ordered to
Scout the road that day? ans. yes. Were you
ordered to ride towards town? ans yes. Did you
order him to Scout the road towards the Still house?
ans. yes. Did you consider him off of his Post
when at the Still House? ans. No. Re-examined
by Judge advocate. Was the Still-House on the
road? ans yes. Re-examined by Apt
Devenport. Do you know where Dobins got
the whiskey? ans. no.

                        his
                     G. H. × Blanch
                       mark

Testimony of Robt Cannon, Questioned by
Judge advocate. Were you on Picket duty with
Iams Dobins? ans. no. Did you see him intoxicated yesterday? ans. I supposed he was.
Where were you when you met him? ans. about
½ mile from town. Did you have any conversation with him? ans. no.
                       R. M. Cannon

Testimony of Eli Philips private in Co. F.
Questioned by Judge advocate. Were you out
on Picket with Iams Dobins yesterday? ans no.
Did you see Mr Dobins yesterday evening? ans yes
after dark. Was he intoxicated when you saw him?
ans. I do not know.

Testimony of Sol. Cerner private in comp. "F"
Questioned by Judge Advocate. Did you see
James Dobins yesterday? Ans. yes. Where was he?
Ans. on his line of duty. Were you on Picket duty
with him? Ans. yes. Where did he get his whiskey?
Ans. at the Still House. Cross examined by
Adjt. Davenport. Was the Still House close to
the road where you were ordered to Scout?
Ans. yes at the end of the line.
                                    Soldier Sworn
Testimony of J.G. Davenport private in Co "F"
Questioned by Judge Advocate, Did you see
James Dobins yesterday evening? Ans yes —
Was he intoxicated? Ans I do not know —
Testimony of W.F. Hale in Co. "F" Questioned
by Judge Advocate, Did you see James
Dobins yesterday? Ans. yes.   Was he
intoxicated? Ans. I do not know —
Testimony of Sm. Bitner private in Co "F"
Questioned by Judge Advocate, Did you
see James Dobins yesterday evening? Ans yes —
Was he intoxicated? Ans I do not know. I never
spoke to him —
            Verdict of the court is guilty of the
Charge. The penalty that he stand on extra
duty alternately for three nights.
   Signed Honorary Capt. Lieut R.F. Sloan judge ad.
                           Approved J.F. White col.
                                        commd.g of Reg.

           Charges against Wm Dobins —
1st For becoming intoxicated while on Picket
duty. 2nd Leaving his Post without any authority
from any officer having charge of the Picket, and

3rd For interrupting the property of citizens and otherwise conducting himself in a manner prejudicial to the good order and discipline of the army of the Con. S. A.

Wm Dolins pleas not guilty.

Testimony of G. H. Blanchet private in Co "F." Questioned by Judge Advocate.

Did you see Wm Dolins on Picket line on yesterday evening? ans Yes. Was he intoxicated? ans yes. Where was he at that time? ans at Sharps on the Clinton road. Was he on Picket duty? ans yes. Did he leave his line of duty? ans No. Did he interupt the person or property of any individual? ans No. Was he conducting himself in a quiet manner? ans No. How was he conducting himself? ans he was laughing and talking to the other boys.

G. H. † Blanchet
his mark

Testimony of Tolver Crews private in Co F. Questioned by Judge Advocate. Were you on Picket yesterday with Wm Dolins? ans yes. Was he intoxicated? ans yes. Was he off his line of Picket duty? ans No. What was he doing while intoxicated? ans he was walking about laughing and talking. Did you see him disturbing any private property belonging to citizens? ans No. Was he conducting himself prejudicial to good order? ans he was not.

Tolver Crews

Verdict of the court Guilty of the Charge. The penalty that he stand on extra duty alternately for three nights.

J. G. Montgomery   Lieut R. F. Sloan
Capt 1st Ky Cavy   Judge Advocate
and Presdt of the court   Approved
                           J. F. White Lieut Col
                              Comndg

Spl ord no 35   Head Quarters 1st R T Cav
                                   Jacksboro Mar 11 1862

2nd Lieut Sloan Co "K" will take a
detachment of 15 men and scout on the mountain
and Huntsville road observing closely for evidence
of the presence of the enemy or his pickets. He will
report at Head Quarters on his return —
                            By order of J F White Lt Col
                                    M Davenport Adjt

                        Head Quarters 1st R T Cav
                                 Mar 11" 1862

Lieut S. C. Wheeler has leave of absence
from company and is relieved of company duties until
the 25th Inst. at the expiration of which time
he will report himself at Head Quarters for duty.
                                J F White Lieut Col

Special order no 36   Head Quarters 1 Reg Tenn Cav
                          Jacksborough 11 March 1862
Commanding officer Comp (F)
                          Will on the arrival of the
provision train from Knoxville make requisition &
draw 5 days additional rations will apply to
quartermaster for transportation camp and equipage
and at as early a date as possible will move
detachment of his Co such men as will best
enable him to cover all of the mountain crossings
of the same. He will arrest all renegades
from East Tenn who are enroute for Ky
disarming them and send the Ringleaders
to. He will will scout daily in all
directions reporting by couriers to these

Head Quarters   By Order of
                              J. F. White Lt Col
                                   Commanding

Special Order No. 37.
                Head Quarters 1st R T Cav
                Savannah Mar 11th 1862

Philo Shepherd is hereby appointed Regimental Steward for First Regt Tenn Cavalry. He will at once enter upon the duties of his office, reporting to the Surgeon for duty.
                By Order of
                J. F. White Lieut Col
M. Davenport, Adjt.

        Head Quarters 1 Reg Ten cavalry
                11 March 1862

Lieut James Wheler has leave of absence from camp and is relieved from camp duties till the 25th of month at which time he will report to Regt Head Quarters for duty.
                J. F. White
                Lt Col

Gen'l Order No. 6
        Head Qutrs 1 Reg Tn Cav Mar 12th 1862
In accordance to instructions and orders rec'd from Head Quarters there will be no more furloughs from Camp only upon Surgeons certificate of disability.
                By Order of
                J. F. White Lieut Col
                    Comg

Special Ord No 38 Head Qrs 1st Rgt T Cavalry
Jacksboro Mar 13 1862

Capt Brown Lieut Atkinson & Lieut Brittain are hereby appointed as a board of Survey to value the horses belonging to the company of Capt A. J. Brock in the Regt Tenn Cavalry

By order of J. F. White Lt Col
M. Davenport Adjt.

Spl Ordr No 39 March 13th 1862

Lieut Baker of "E" Lieut R. F. Sloan and Lieut F. P. Sloan both of Co "I" will meet immediately in committee to examine certain bacon bought by the Quarter master, which was issued to certain companies, and returned, and report to these Head quarters.

By Order of
J. F. White Lieut Col

Jacksboro Tenn March 13 1862

We the undersigned committee of the 1st Rgt Tenn Cavalry having made the necessary examination find 773 lbs of bacon that is unfit for use in the Commissary department.

Lieut R. F. Sloan Co "I"
F. P. Sloan " "
John Baker " "E"

Head Quarters 1st Regt Ten Corp
Spel Ordr No 40.   Jacksboro March 1st 1863

Lieut McMahan will take a detail of 8 men from comp. E and the comdr of comps. I will detail 7 men to ~~start~~ go with him, Start at 15 minuets after 2 oclock PM and Scout the Huntsville Road 2 or three miles out beyond the top of the Mountain.

By Ordr of
Capt J.G.W. Montgomery
Comndr of Post.

Head Qtrs 1 Rgt Tenn Cav
Jacksboro Mar 1st

Hd Qrs Kingston Tenn
May 31st 1862 —

Genl Order
No. 3 } John S. Oneal, will act as Qr. Master
for the 7 Regt Tenn Cav. and the various officers
Non. comd Off. & privates of that Command
and the Regt Qr. Mastr will give him the
respect & obedience becoming his position.

Sm. B. McLin Major —
Comdg Post —

HdQrs Kingston Ten
June 9th 1862 —

Genl Order
No. 4 } Commanders of Companies of this
Regt. will have their tents Stricked, and
Stored in some Suitable & safe place under
direction of the Qr. Mastr of the Regt, except-
ing tents & Flies for a Company, and be
ready to move the whole Command by 9 Oclock
A.M. tomorrow into their encamp-
ment said Co. & flies to the Col. and all their
Garrison equipage. They will move to the left of the
location of the Gen. Hdqs, near Kentuck firm
and camp together & encampment

Hd Qrs Kingston Tenn
June the 8th 1862

Special Order }
No }

The Commanders of Companies now with their Companies with energy and decision will see that each man of his Company cleans up and see that his gun is in the best shooting condition in which he can place it, that his Saber belt &c is at hand; that each man is provided with ten rounds of ammunition, haversack, ball pouch, powder flask, bridle, saddle, blanket, and all a Soldier accoutrements to place each man to do. Tell to that in few minds they will be ready to obey any order to scout, fight or whatnot without being in one anothers way and without confusion. This order must be obeyed

Most Respectfully
John. B. McLin Col
Commanding Post

Hd Qrs Kingston 8th
June the 8th 1862

General Order }
No }

Hd Qrs 1st Regt Tenn Cav'l
Camp Allston Near Kingston, June 18th 1862

Order No 5
Commanders of Companies will see that there is no Horse Racing by their Men any violation of this order Commanders of Companies of Companies will immediately arrest the parties and bring them to these Hd Qrs or they themselves will be held responsible.
By Order of
Lt Col Comdg Regt
E A Broyles Actg Adjt

Hd Qrs 1st Regt Tenn Cav
Camp Allston June 22nd 1862

Orders No
All officers and Soldiers *illegible*

illegible section

Hd Qrs 1st Regt Tenn Cavalry
Camp Allston Kingston Tenn
July 1st 1862

Orders
The Commander of each Company of the Companies of this Regt at this place will have their Companies with all their Clothing utentiles, one tent and two files of each Company and six days unprepared rations all packed and in their wagons (which will be furnished by the Qr Master) Horses Saddled and ready to mount and march at 12 Oclock A.M.

The Commander of each Company will be expected to see that every man of his Company, march not only in Column but in regular order and promptly closed up. Ten oclock not not eleven is must in this order. By Order of

Jno B McLin Col
Comdg Regt

R F Sloan
Acting Adjutant

Hd Qrs 1st Regt Tenn Cavalry
Camp near Maynardsville Tenn July 4th 1862

Special Order
No ___

At Seven Oclock A.M. tomorrow the Commanders of the Companies of this Regt will each be ready to move with his entire Company and at the command of a Regimental Officer will form be thrown into regular Column and March Compact across the creek to our newly selected Camping ground in the woods. The Companies will be encamped in ___ line in the order of their Letters Company B on the right. Each Company will dig sinks front of the center of their encampment, which must be the place of burial ___ for the men, that our beautiful and cheap cooks be not made sick by ___ least exposure. There will be a due observance of the rules of the field and Staff Officers. The reveille roll call will be sounded at day light twenty minutes after which the Ob Adjutant if the army ___ under direction of Commanding officer without one moment's delay will commence calling the roll marking the absentees; Immediately thereafter stable call will be sounded, when the Commanders of Companies will see that the Companies proceed immediately to water feed curry and rub their Horses thoroughly under the Supervisions of a Sargent of the Company who will see that the men move off regularly to and from water and keep properly closed. The N.C. Officers having charge of Squads will See that all the Horses of their Squad are watered at that time if possible one man can ride a horse and lead three if members of the Squad are absent or incapable of taking care of their horse

Surgeon's Call will be Sounded at 5½ Oclock A.M. when the Sick will be conducted by the 1st Sargents of the Companies to the Surgeons Quarters

Drill Call will be Sounded at 6 Oclock A.M. when the Commanders of Companies will See that all their men present for duty turn out dismounted none will be excused from drill except those excused by the Surgeon dismounted drill from 6 to 8 Oclock. Officers Call will be Sounded at 9 Oclock A.M. when all the officers will assemble at Regt. Hd. Qrs. for drill and instruction for two hours. Water Call will be Sounded at 10 Oclock A.M. Drill Call for N.C. officers will be Sounded at 2 Oclock P.M. when all N.C. Officers not on other duty will be assembled at Regimental Hd. Qrs. and be instructed and drilled under the directions and Supervisions of the Comdg. Officer of the Regt. N.C. officer drill from 2 to 4 Oclock P.M. Water Call will be Sounded at 3 Oclock P.M. Drill Call will be Sounded at 4 Oclock P.M. when Companies will turn out mounted. Stable Call will be Sounded at 6 Oclock P.M. Dress parade at Sundown. Tattoo roll call will be Sounded at 8½ Oclock P.M. Taps at 9 Oclock when all lights will be extinguished and all noise and confusion in camp Suppressed

Not more than five men from each Company will be allowed to be absent from camps at once they to have a permit Signed by the Commander of

Officer of the Company and countersigned by the Adjutant of the Regiment

II ~~Commander of Companies~~ Call for guard mounting will be sounded at 8 Oclock A M when the details for guard will be conducted to the Regimental parade Ground by the 1st Sergeants of Companies. Horses may be watered opposite the front of their encampment in the nearest branch but never higher up the branch which must be kept clean for culinary purposes. ~~So much of the foregoing calls except~~ require their ~~much as and immediate~~ Compliance

There will be Company inspection of arms (Guns & Sabers) by Company Commanders every Sabbath Morning and they are expected to be kept bright and in as good repair as practable. All guns that have not been recently inspected will have the loads drawn from them immediately and the guns cleaned out thoroughly and put in good ~~fix~~ All guns from which the load cannot be drawn will be brought and reported to 28th Reg't

Commanders of Companies will have opened in front of their encampments broad and convenient passages to water & if need be one man can ride a horse and lead them. In connection with each Company encampment there will be cleaned up and handsomely ~~laid out~~ a Company parade Ground

The Commanders of Companies and their assistence will be expected to see that their NC Officers having charge of squads have the arms and equipments of each squad kept together and seperate from those of the other men for the purpose of securing order and promptness

Most Respectfully
Jos. B. McLin Col
Comg. Reg.

Hd Qrs 2nd Regt Tenn Cav
Special Orders   Camp Maynardsville Tenn July 12. 1862
No

          Private ____ in Comp "K" of this
Regt is hereby appointed forage master for the Same
and all his Legitimate and lawful Orders and acts
connected with the Same Shall be respected as the same
                    By Order of
                         Jno. B. McLin Col
                              Comdg Regt

                         Hd Qrs 2nd Regt Tenn Cav
                         Maynardsville Tenn July 16, 1862
Special Orders
No

          Capt Mims will report immediately
to Major Clay A. A. G. at Knoxville
                    By Order of
                         Jno. B. McLin Col
                              Comdg Regt

                         Hd Qrs 2nd Regt Tenn Cavl
                         Maynardsville July 18th 1862
Lt Col. McKenzie
          Will go immediately and discover
where the four Companies of this Regt recently stationed
at Walless X Roads Cos E, F, G & H now are. Take
command of the Same. Conduct them back to
Walless X Roads and guard and defend that pass
discover the advance of any enemy from the
mountains into Powles Valley, all along the line
between Walless X Roads and Fincastle inclusive
and report to these Hd Qrs immediately and to
Dept Hd Qrs Knoxville all the orders heretofore
issued to Capt Blackwell and Mims

will be faithfully obeyd all that may be of importance to the publick service

Lt. Carter with his command will shortly relieve Lt Col McKenzie and the companies above alluded to shortly at which time Lt Col McKenzie and his command will promptly move to Musters ford of Clinch and report to Col Ashby for Orders. Most Respectfully

Jno B. McLin
Comdg Regt

Hd Qrs 2nd Regt Tenn Cvlr
Moynordsville Tenn July 20/

Special Order
No.

Capt W.O. Martin will take command of his whole company that are capable of service officers and privates with one days pre-pared rations and be ready to march with blankets precisely at 8 oclock P.M. when Capt Tom will report to their Hd Qrs for further instructions

By Command of
Col Jno. B. McLin
Comdg Regt

Hd Qrs 2nd Regt Tenn Cvlr
Moynordsville Tenn July 20/

The Commanders of each of the comp's will report to their Hd Qrs the exact number of men able for duty in case of emergency who were not on the Scout that has just returned or on picket last night

By Order of
Col Jno. B. McLin
Comdg Regt
R.A. Shaw AdC

Hd Qrs 9nd Regt Tenn Cav
Maynardsville July 20/6_

Special Order
No __

S. L. Rogan who has been acting as Sergeant in Com "B" of Said Regt, because of his inefficiency and gross neglect of duty in office is hereby reduced to the rank of a private, and J. D. Blevins of S'd Com is hereby appointed Sergeant in S'd Comp'y and all his acts and orders in this connexion are required to be respected and obeyed. This order will be read to the Com at roll Coll.
                    J. B. McLin Col
                    Com'dg Regt

Hd Qrs 9nd Regt Tenn Cav
Maynardsville Tenn July 22/6_

Special Order
No __

Robert H. Williams, Second Corporal in Comp. B, because of his rebellious and disorderly conduct in refusing to act as Corporal of the guard when detailed for that duty, and insultingly and disrespectfully asserting he would not do so, and for cursing and treating with great disrespect the orderly Sergeant detailing him for that duty, is hereby forbidden from this time forth to act as Corporal in S'd Com, but is hereby reduced to the position of private and Geo. f. McInnis is hereby appointed to the office of 2nd Corporal in S'd Com, and all his legitimate acts and orders in connection therewith are required to be respected and obeyed as such. By Order J. B. McLin Col
                    Com'dg Regt

Hd Qrs 3rd Regt Tenn Cavalry
Moymondville July 31st 1862

Capt Martin V. Biggles

Will immediately make
preperations and by 10 Oclok A.M. march with
their entire Company for Wallaces Cross Roads with
as much Dispatch as practable when they will
picket and scout the ford of Lt Col Corters
position which he has been ordered to leave
for the present. Upon Lt Col Corters return
they will also return to this point.
Lt Col Corter will leave directions as to points
of Pickets and Scouts.

Most Respectfully
J.B. McLin Col
Comdg Regt

P.S. The Quartermaster will furnish
our transportation to the above Compan[y]
J.B. McLin Col

Hd Qrs 2nd Batt Tenn Cav
Camp Hunting Creek Aug 15th 1862

Special Order
No. 1   Capt James M. Martin will proceed to take charge of all the Commissary stores that Capt S. H. Boggus has on hand.

By order of Lt Col G. W. M. Kenzie
R. F. Sloan A Adjt

Genl Order
No. 1   Head Qrs 2 Bat T Cav
         Pine Forge Sept 6"

The following reconstruction in the letters of the cos by this command takes place from this date. Vizt Capt Blackwell's Co. becomes Co "A" Capt Kincaid's "B" Capt Martin's "C" Capt Biglis "D" Capt Carder's "E" Capt Mim's "F" Capt Graham's "G" Capt Mallindore's "H"

By Order of
Lt Col G. W. M. Kenzie
R. F. Sloan Ag

Tenn   occupying   the
        bound
Decatur Tenn Meigs Co
Banishment

Received of N. G. Moss wrong
Received Decatur

(Copy)　　　　　　Head Qrs. 2d Bat. Tenn. Cav.
　　　　　　　　　　Sept 10th 1862

Genl Stevenson
　Comdg 1st Div. Dept. E. Tenn.
　　　　　　Sir
　Rev E. A. Boyles the Bearer of this, and the
Pearp. Major [?] of my command, desires a detail
for the purpose of assisting to make up a company
in Washington Co. Mr Boyles is a very worthy
gentleman, and has an offer of a Lieut. place
in a Co. nearly made up in his county. If you
can grant him the detail, you will benefit the
service & confer a favor on
　J. S. Weeks　　　　Your Obedt Servt
　　　　　　　　　　J. W. McKenzie Col.

If Col. McKenzie's Bat. is full, he can detach
the applicant for the purpose stated; if not I would
suggest to him to use his competent officers or
men to fill his ranks.
　　　　　　　　　　C. L. Stevenson
　John Weeks　　　　　Brig Genl
　　　　　　　　　　Comdg
J S Weeks

　　　　　　Head Qrs. 2d Bat. Tenn Cav.
　　　　　　　Knoxville Sept 12" 1862
By virtue of the authority endorsed on this application, Mr E. A. Boyles herein mentioned, is granted
a special leave of absence for forty days
to proceed to Washington Co. for the purposes mentioned
in this application.　　J. W. McKenzie Lt Col
　　　　　　　　　　Comdg Bat.

Hd Qtrs 3rd Battalion Tenn Cav
Sept 15, 1862

Charges & Specifications against Phillip
Merick, private in Capt. Martin's Co. (C) 3d
Battalion Tenn Cav 3d Brigade

Charges

Unsoldierlike conduct.

Specifications

1st Said Phillip Merick was regularly detailed
on the 9th of Sept 1862 for picket duty, and
whilst on post did disgracefully leave & desert
his post without permission, contrary to Army
Regulations & Articles of War.

E. O. Martin Capt
Co. (C) 3d Bat T Cav

Witnesses:
Corpl. T. F. Wood
Private D. B. Nance

Hd Qrs 2nd Bat Tenn Cav
Kingston Nov 14th 1862

Capt J. M. Kincaid
Sir
You will proceed on Saturday
the 15th inst between the hours of 1 & 2 oclock P.M. & hold
an election in your Co. for a first & 2d Lieut to fill the vacan-
cies now existing.

J. M. Montgomery Major
Comdg 2nd Bat Tenn Cav

Hd Qr 2nd Batt Tenn Cav
Camp near Kingston Nov 18th 1862

Capt. J. M. Kincaid
Sir
You will proceed on Tuesday the 18th inst. to open & hold between the hours of 10 O'clock A.M. & 12 M. to open & hold an election in your company for an act. 2nd Lieut. to fill the vacancy therein existing.

By order of G W McKenzie Lt Col
Comdg Batt
R. H. Sloan Adjt

Hd Qr. 2nd Batt Tenn Cavalry
Camp near Kingston Tenn
Nov. 18th 1862

James A. Day is hereby appointed Steward of the 2nd Batt. Tenn. Cavalry, and will rank as such.

Samj H. Day Surgeon
2nd Batt Tenn Cavalry

Approved
G. W. McKenzie Lt Col.
Comdg 2nd Batt Tenn Ca
R. H. Sloan
Adjt.

Hd Qr 2nd Batt Tenn Cavalry
Camp near Kingston Nov 18th 1862

Special Order

An Election having been held on the 18th Nov. 1862 in accordance with orders W L Musick receiving majority is declared elected and is assigned to duty as Brevt 2nd Lieut. Co (B) 2nd Batt Tenn Cavalry

By order of Lt Col G W McKenzie Comdg
R. H. Sloan Adjt

Hd Qrs 5th Regt Tenn Cav
Camp near Knoxville, Jany 5th 1862

The Commander of Co. (C) will detail Jno. E. McCarty to report to the A.Q.M. for duty as forage Master

By order G. W. McKenzie Col.
Comdg Regt
P. F. Sloan Adjt

Hd Qrs 5th Regt Tenn Cav.
Lenoirs, Jan. 13th 1863.

General Orders No. 7

1st. The commanders of companies have no authority to furlough, detail, or order any N.C. officer or private away from the regt.

2d. All commanders of companies are required to arrest & prefer written charges & specifications against every N.C. officer or private who may be absent without leave, and all those who have absented themselves a second time since the army came out of Kentucky.

3d. Any failure on the part of company commanders to comply with the above orders, the law in all its rigor will be enforced against such officers.

By order
G. W. McKenzie Col.
Comdg 5th Regt Tenn Cav
P. F. Sloan Adjt

Hd Qrs 3rd Regt Tenn Cavalry
Maynardsville Tenn Feb 11th 1863

Capt A J Ragan
 Comdg Co. A 3rd Regt Tenn Cav

You will proceed to hold an election in your company at 9 Oclock tomorrow morning to elect a Brevet 2nd Lt the vacancy having occured by the promotion of Capt J L Blackwell to Major of 3rd Regt Tenn Cav

G W M Kenzie Col
Comdg 3rd Regt Tenn Cav

Hd Qrs 3rd Regt Tenn Cav
Maynardsville Feb 12th 1863

In obedience to an order of Col G W M Kenzie Comdg 3rd Regt I proceeded to hold an election for Brevet 2nd Lt in my Company the result of the election is as follows:

M D Lansford being the only candidate Recd thirty six votes

Signed G W Gardner Clerk

I Certify that the above is a true return of an election held in my Co for Brevet 2nd Lt at 9 Oclock A M Feb 12th 1863

Signed A J Ragan Capt
Comdg Company

The said M D Lansford is hereby ordered to report to Capt A J Ragan for duty

By order
G W M Kenzie Col
Comdg 3rd Regt Tenn Cav

R H Sloan
Adjt

Hd Qrs 3d Regt Tenn Cav
Camp near Knoxville Feby 28th 1863

Special Order }
No. 3 } Capt A.J. Ragan & Lt. S.H. Wilson of Co. A
and Lt. W.L. Horner of Co. (B) is hereby appointed a
Board of survey to value a horse that was killed in
action near Harrodsburg K.Y. belonging to private James
Taylor of Co. D 1st Regt Tenn Cav. and report their action
to these Hd Qrs.   By order C.M. M.Kenzie Col
                    Comdg 3rd Regt Tenn Cav
                         N.E. Sloan Adjt

In obedience to the above order we the undersigned
Board of survey after due consultation and with a
personal knowledge of the said horse do agree and
value the said horse at One hundred & Twenty five
Dollars
                         A.J. Ragan Capt
                         S.H. Wilson Lt
                         W.L. Horner Lt

        Hd Qrs 3d Rc.

            You
Received Decatur April 1st 1877 $ 61.25 for
            Received S.S.H.D.

C.M. M.Kenzie

Hd Qrs 5d Regt Tenn Cav
Camp near Knoxville Feb 28th 1863

Capt. A. J. Mason

You will proceed at once to muster & inspect Capt Carders Co (E) for the months of Jany & Feb 1863

By order J L Blackwell Maj
Cmdg Regt

N H Sloan Adjt

Hd Qrs 5d Regt Tenn Cav
Camp near Knoxville Feb 28th 1863

Capt D. M. Carder

You will proceed at once to muster & inspect the following Cos viz Cos A, B, C, D, F, G, H, I, & K for the months of Jany & Feb 1863

By order J L Blackwell Maj
Cmdg Regt

Yours very respectfully N H Sloan Adjt

Decatur Tenn
Feb 12 1877

Mr. John Croft

Dear Sir We received your kind letter

Yours very respectfully

Yours very respectfully
J C W—

A Bond for one peacon, with a condition
Know all men by these presents, that I, G. C. McK.
of the city of Decatur state of Tenn bind my self
to pay

Yours very   47
                         40)700)17
Clay, Calhoun, Webster   Proverbs XV 2   41 529
                                         30 4
                                         280 23½
                                          20 82½

The tongue of the wise useth knowledge right
Critical Period of Ago 24 Par 3
the slavery trouble
Monroe's Administration. Admission of Mo. 2
Clays efforts passed the Missouri Compromise.
North wanted a free state her own people wanted slaves
South 36°30' the states determined for themselves

                    Jackson 1828
Disunion threatened. Separate the Navy S
Protective Tariff Hayne and Calhoun Nullifiers
Webster on the other side. Clay an arbitrator.
I would rather be right than President. Jackson
                                          ordered
                                          troops
Wilmot Proviso lost Run Ex Pres Van Buren
Free Soilers

Head Quarters Army (Tennessee)
Dalton, Ga. March 30 1864

General Orders }
No 28 } I. In pursuance of an act of Congress entitled "An Act to provide for retiring officers of the Army" published in G.O. 26 A.D.I.G.O. 1864 which authorizes the President of the Confederate States upon the recommendation of the General Commanding to "discharge from service any officer who has no command & cannot be assigned to any appropriate duty, or who is incompetent or inefficient, or who may be absent from his command or duty without leave" Commanding Officers will report the names of such officers as come within its perview and forward their reports to these Hd qrs with the remarks of intermediate Commanders — fairly & fully presenting each case

II. Each name will be reported on a separate paper and will state the grade Company and Regiment or Battalion of the officer; If absent, by what authority & where he may be found; and if absent on duty, what duty & by whose order he may have been assigned

III. In order that the army may be speedily relieved of incompetent & unworthy officers it is important that these reports should be made promptly

By Command of General Johnston
(sg) Kinlock Falconer
AAG

Official
Capt E.S. Burford
AAG

Official
J.W.S. Grierson Jr
AAAG

Hd Qrs Humes Brigade
Tunnel Hill Ga April 2 1864

The reports called for in Genl Orders
No 28 Hd qrs Army Tenn, dated Dalton
Ga March 30 1864 — will be forwarded
without delay to these Hd qrs

By Order of
Brig Genl Humes
J W Frierson Jr
a a a g

Col G W McKenzie
Comdg 5 Tenn Cav